Deep Truth

Wisdom of the Masters
Reality and Illusion

Practical steps to understand the Universe, master the mind, develop intuition, deepen wisdom & live an inspired life!

Jean Walters, DM, DD, CRT

Deep Truth

Wisdom of the Masters
Reality and Illusion

Practical steps to understand the Universe,
master the mind, develop intuition,
deepen wisdom & live an inspired life!

ISBN: 978-0-9979375-5-8

Cover Design by Anne Cote and Layne Walker
Cover photo: iStock 494839291, Licensed to Layne Walker

Published October 2021
Inner Connections Publishing
St. Louis, Mo

Welcome Reader

Thank you for your support in purchasing this book. It is my great joy to share this information with you that you may live an exalted life of freedom and peace.

Please check my video library on youtube.com which promises to instruct you in universal laws, meditation techniques, and personal empowerment. By understanding these principles and applying them to your life, you become the master of your destiny and open to greater awareness and possibilities. May you be enriched through these writings.

Dedication

I dedicate this book to all the great teachers that have impacted my life. That includes an endless list because everyone I know, my family, friends, students, clients and collaborators, has enlarged my life and awareness in some way and I am so grateful!

May you find your wisdom in these pages!

Acknowledgements

As Spirit is my guide, I live a life of abundance and joy as I am continuously supplied with people who know how to do the things that I don't know how to do and resources that provide the next step.

Included in this list of talented folks is my good friend and collaborator, Anne Cote, who is an editor and book cover designer extraordinaire. I love working with her because 1) she gets what I am trying to say and 2) as our collaboration develops it becomes a stream of creative energy flowing rhythmically between us and, …quite magically a book emerges. I am always thrilled with our result.

Another great talent who brings his years of book publishing to the project is Layne Walker. You see Layne's expertise in the cover art as well and the book interior design. He is a master of his craft.

Of course there are others who offer their specialty, expertise and lots of encouragement - coaches and teachers, and technical wizards. Thank you for holding my hand.

For forty years I have been privileged to bring the words of the masters to many thousands of people through my classes, YouTube videos, counseling sessions, books and lectures. It has been a tremendous honor to walk with them as they grew and expanded. It is my knowing that as each person adds his drop of love, brilliance, and compassion into the quantum field, we all benefit by experiencing a kinder, more loving world. That is what I am most grateful for – that I got to do this and you get to do this too!

Table of Contents

Foreword

My Story - How It All Began

> *One of the preoccupations of people throughout all times and all cultures have been to find that which is sacred, which is transcendental, which is beyond the small sense of self, our jobs and relationships, this small I. In all cultures, this search is taken as a journey of a yogi, a healer, a shaman, a seer or wise person. Although separate by continents and centuries, it is always the same journey. It is the journey of going from the small self-centered view of the world to an awareness of its vastness and mystery.*
>
> Jack Kornfield

I have been at this study to connect, to achieve greater awareness, and to understand the transcendent reality in which we live for a long time. It seems that each person wakes up at some point with an understanding, an awareness of what it is that drives one. In my, case it came early. I wanted to fathom how people knew what it was they were to become? How did they know? Of course, behind that question was another one: *How am I to know?*

I pondered that question because something inside of me knew that I was not to be "normal." What I mean by that is, what I saw to be normal (in my child's perception) was that people went to work every day to make money so that they could pay the bills, live in a house, and someday retire. I didn't get it. It made no sense to me. It seemed ridiculous. It depressed me.

Then, one day, I was speaking to my high school drivers-education teacher, and I told him of my consternation that I couldn't see how I could live the life I just described. I didn't know what to do.

He saw my quandary and did something miraculous. He drew a circle. It was just a line drawn into a circle. He said, "See this space within the circle? It represents everything you know, and this line that is drawn around that inner space (the periphery of the circle) represents everything you don't know. Now, look what happens when you expand what you know. The line around the circle also expands."

In a few brief minutes, he gave me purpose. He showed me that, no matter how much I learned, there would be more that I didn't know. There would always be more to explore and understand. He gave me a reprieve. I didn't' have to live anyone else's life. I could live my own life. I felt the weight come off my shoulders. I felt myself breathing again. It was a start. I had a purpose!

Since that time, I have thought about my teacher and his circle. I plunged (literally) into spirituality early in life. I wanted to know. How does the Universe work? I knew intuitively it wasn't happenstance, but that wasn't enough. I wanted to know HOW it worked, what I could depend upon, how to trust it. That was the quest…and I did it!

I learned and grew and practiced. I went into my laboratory (myself) and experimented to see if I could create the life I wanted. I did this repeatedly because I wanted to see what was real, what I could count on.

That has been my life's work. And then I taught it, spoke about it, wrote about it, and shared it. Other people found the same stability that I did. That is how this book came into existence. I wanted to share this knowledge because I know it is the thing you can count on also, the one stable truth.

The interesting fact is that Truth does not change. The material world changes, moment by moment, but truth does not change. That is what you will come to terms with in these pages.

I have stories illustrating the points I make. I have outlined exercises and techniques so that you could find your own truth, because my truth is not enough for you. You must find your own. But don't worry. Truth does not vary. It is always constant. That is what you will discover: truth, stability, practices, and concepts to challenge you and make your own.

It is my joy to share this information, and just like my drivers-education teacher, I hope you are able to draw your own circle and keep filling it with understanding so that you can expand beyond all imagined boundaries and understand that the only thing that frees you is *Truth.*

On occasion in this treatise, I will make reference to *A Course in Miracles*. This Course is composed of spiritually channeled material. It provides information as to the process of returning your consciousness to the original guilelessness and openness of a child capable of learning anything and placing no limitations upon the self. As such, it is a guide to dissolving the ego, that man-made sense of identity with the material form and worldly pronouncements. The value of performing the exercises outlined in *A Course* is that, without the ego, one begins to see the world in new light.

My desire is that you explore the practices outlined and develop mental discipline and strength, the ability to fix on your objective (goal) until it is manifest. I also wish for you the peace that accompanies mental control.

In the offing, I offer great appreciation to all who choose to travel this path of self-mastery. This is how we will change the world. We were made to be the masters of our fate. Now is the time!

Introduction

What This Book Is About

You Shall know the truth and the truth shall set you free.
John 8:32

The truth offered in this book has been around forever, but few recognize how it operates in their lives. It is not that they don't have the ability to understand these principles, because they do. They can also apply this truth in practical ways in everyday situations to master life and live in a joyful state, but many won't do that.

Most folks don't seek the truth and therefore they don't find it. Often, they go through life not noticing anything around them, as they are brain-soaked in their little world of worries and frustrations. However, there are wondrous things peeking out through nooks and crannies, and adventures ready to be had. Perhaps that is what you will find: a way to ignite your inner torch and motivation to begin a new chapter. That is my wish.

This book is not about intellectual achievement. It is about the heart or soul. The heart is the pathway to the soul. The soul is your connection to Infinity (God). It is about living from your heart. The way to mastership is through the heart. You must feel your way through life. To live fully, you must return to the innocence and wonder of a child, because little ones, being fresh and open, see with wonder, enthusiasm and joy. They are not caught up in a small material world that they cannot see beyond, and that is why Jesus said to enter the kingdom as a child.

In life, there are messages everywhere, and when we become

sensitive enough to see, feel, and acknowledge them, we become wise. That is the point when we will know for sure that there is something magical happening within and about us, no matter what appears to be going on in our small field of human vision.

In this book, I will discuss the way the Universe works (flows) and practical methods to direct universal law and principles: magnetism, deep listening, connecting to our inner Light and life purpose, among other things. This information is offered with the objective of handing you the reins to your life. What do you want? Are you ready to take charge?

Life is a beautifully woven tapestry containing the texture and design of the intentions of those who helped to weave it with their vision, determination, actions, and yearnings. Each thread is magnificently placed. As you read, you will recognize the intricacy of your tapestry and how your life plays out within its framework. You will walk away with tools to go forward and fulfill your greater purpose.

When practiced, the information in this book will guide you to mastery. You no longer have to fuss and moan over outcomes that go beyond your power to change or understand. You will know when to stop and when to move forward. Perhaps you will recognize your divine uniqueness and gifts.

Each person is placed in the earth to fulfill a divine mission, to grow and add to the whole. How to do this? When to move forward and when to hold back? You have the answers. You must look in your heart. That is where you will find access to your soul.

In this book, we delve deep into consciousness (energy/life) to bring forth the truth that sets you free. Access this deep wisdom and the world opens to you.

Every Person Is a Unique Part of the Whole

We are living art, created to hang on, stand up, forbear, continue, and encourage others.
Maya Angelou

Just as a snowstorm is composed of millions of snowflakes, man is an individualized particle of God, the Quantum Field. Just as a human child is an expression of its earthly parents, you are an expression of your divine parent. As you grow in understanding your Spiritual Source, you will mirror your inherent divinity and expand in creativity and expression. There is no limit to what is possible. The ultimate quest is to expand your Spiritual Father-child relationship, and that means to grow in knowing!

The Bible indicates the Father (God, the Quantum Field) as stating, *"Everything I have is yours*." This statement reveals that, as a divine offspring, you have the same qualities and attributes as your Father. (You are made in His image). The simple truth: you are made in God energy. Mark 4:4: *You are God.* It is thus your assignment to develop your capabilities to full measure as you proceed.

The Biblical quote is this*: If anyone sheds the blood of man, by man shall his blood be shed: for in the image of God has man been made.* Genesis 9:6

This passage points out man's important position in God's kingdom because *made in the image of God* does not pertain to physical attributes of God, but that we have the same power, energy, and qualities of the Father, and it is up to each one to develop this potential into practical usage that one may take ownership of one's own divinity.

Jesus said, "In a word, you must be made perfect as your heavenly Father is perfect." Matthew 5:48 We are to demonstrate our divinity through words and actions. We are to be the highest expression of love.

Each person must choose how he is to *be in his Father's house.* Or, in what way he is to connect with and express his divine heritage. We not only channel this high energy of love, but we surrender to it as well. In this way, we can learn through each experience, challenge and possibility. We can connect to our Greater Self through the still small voice of intuition and receive the guidance and comfort needed in each moment.

Each job, relationship, situation, experience and adventure offer something new to explore and from which to learn. A growth-oriented person approaches opportunities with excitement. Even death, regardless of human opinion, is a new beginning and can be perceived as completion of one experience and the beginning of another one. This is true for both the one transitioning and those left behind.

Life is nothing but a series of experiences to expand creativity, grow in wisdom, and influence with love. Commitment to be in the Father's house comes at different times and in different forms for each person. It is about intention and focus. Each person arrives in his own time. Nevertheless, as we take each step along the journey, we can feel our sonship (oneness) with the Father – the Presence of God – the Quantum Field of Love. We are in It and of It. It is behind every experience and It completely supports you!

The Simple Vast Truth

The most beautiful experience we can have is the mysterious –
the fundamental emotion which stands at the cradle
of true art and true science.
Albert Einstein

The science of Quantum Physics has determined that there is but one energy in the Universe. This energy in which we live, breathe, and have our being has various names: the Quantum Field, Holographic Field, and the Unified Field to name a few. Some people even call it God. An analogy for this vast field of energy would be the ocean. In its vastness, the ocean touches and supplies in some form or other all life. If the ocean dies, we all perish.

The ocean contains millions of waves, each one rising for the moment and then subsiding as its time passes. Each wave swells as a temporary form out of a constant medium: the ocean. No matter what, the ocean, whether active or silent, continues. It pays no heed to the number of waves rising on its surface or the multitude of life forms inhabiting its depth. It moves rhythmically while effortlessly abiding shelter to millions of species and life forms. It shifts and flows without fret or concern, fulfilling its mission as an energy and field of liquid wonder.

Individuals are like waves in the ocean. Each person is born into the ocean of life, illustrating certain characteristics. On the surface, they all appear separate, yet in their deepest selves, and always, they are the same. Some reflect big, ebullient qualities, while others display timidity. Some are loud or violent and others quiet and subtle. One ascends and another submerges. Yet, the constant behind all individuals is the same. On the outside they appear independent, but when examined in depth, they are composed of the same element, the same energy, the quantum field. Thus, all are connected.

A person dies and another is born. How can they be connected? Yet, each one is an extension of the last. The new one gathers energy (knowledge, wisdom) from those passing before. We are never living in the same world, only the same substance.

As individuals complete their earthly sojourns, they make way for new entities to enter. The original persons' contributions have prepared a world with just the right components, events, and energy for the next ones to arrive and do their work and make their contributions. You might say, we gather energy from those who have gone before. Certainly, we are living in a different world than the one inhabited by Martin Luther King, Jr., Thomas Edison, or Abraham Lincoln. Did their contributions make way for your message or involvement?

No matter if you are in the earth for a day or a decade or more, you leave your mark in a variety of ways. From the wisdom and love you share, there are many ripples across the stream of life. The point is that, by being present at a particular time, you have contributed. You have supported the next wave of invention or transformation. In the Universe, nothing is wasted. All find their way to affect life in their unique design and purpose.

Individuals influence others through support and advice, or education and nurturing. Whether you know it or not, you are supplying substance for the creation of the next wave or generation. It is an on-going cycle and one uniquely built according to all that has gone before.

It may seem like we are individuals, but that is an illusion. Each person is but a tiny form, appearing in the vast ocean of universal consciousness. From the point of view of form, we appear unique and individual. Yet, behind the form, we are the same. Each being rises and falls within this quantum energy and the field remains constant (just like the ocean). The duality that appears to be a wave and an ocean is not so. They are connected and we are the same: waves in a cosmic ocean. Non-duality, or oneness, is the reality.

Each person has a choice to view the self as an individual or to focus deeper to the commonality of Spirit. We live in a vast ocean of Spirit, each one demonstrating different talents, strengths, and weaknesses. When we connect with our deepest truth, who we really are, our true selves, we are as vast as the ocean, and just as powerful.

We have been given everything we need. We have the ability to relax into Spirit and recognize our inherent magnificence. It is the truth of who we are. It is how we connect to all that is. To go deeper into the self, to the vastness of being, accept that you are alive in an unlimited field of energy. This is how you can practice.

Shut your eyes and close down your sensory perceptions: hearing, seeing, touch, smell, taste. Be quiet in the present moment and watch your breath inspire and expire in its natural rhythm. Take a moment and marvel at the miracle of breath. Stay in this awareness for a few minutes.

Notice that, as you observe your breath, your awareness broadens, and you can sense a deeper, more subtle spaciousness. With practice, you not only become more comfortable in this stillness, but you will find it replenishing. With practice, you will be able to open more fully to the vast inner stillness and your awareness will deepen.

Quantum physicists and spiritual theologians have been coming together in acknowledging this one field of energy. Perhaps it is what Jesus referred to when he was asked, "Where do we find God?" His answer was that we will not find God looking here or looking there (because God is everywhere, the entire ocean of energy in which we live, breathe, and have our being).

As you move into inner stillness, you can surrender to it and become one with it. It will not happen on an intellectual level because it is as Jesus and other spiritually evolved people described: you must enter it by feeling It. This field is in you, around you, and everywhere. Omniscient, omnipresent, omnipotent. Floating in it is analogous to swimming in a vast peaceful ocean.

Practice by standing before the night sky and imagine your mind stretching to take up the entire cosmos. Or, you can imagine being on the top of a mountain and looking out over an expansive territory.

As you gaze, allow yourself to expand into the scene, the clouds, the grass, the trees, and rocks. Open to embrace everything. It is what yogis refer to as being as small as an ant or as vast as an elephant. You let your mind expand to vastness or retract to the world of an ant.

To expand into vastness, you must stabilize in your center. In other words, focus your attention on your center and feel it. It is an area around the solar plexus. As you connect to your center, you can feel the energy around you.

Becoming centered (grounded) is important if you want to experience inner vastness. As you do this, you are letting go of your small material (self) body in order to be the entire ocean or the vast sky. It is freedom.

Chapter 1: The Beginning

Life on Earth - The Process

At any moment, you have a choice that either leads you closer to your Spirit or further away from it.
Nich Nhat Hanh

How did we get here and why are we living this earth life? It is dense, challenging, and not always pleasant. If you've ever had your computer crash, gotten a cold, or been in in an argument, you know the dense, clumsy, restrictive aspect of our material world. And yet there is a reason to be here. And more importantly, it doesn't have to be unpleasant.

There is more to it than meets the eye. The events described above are just outer, external representations of life on earth. We also have the opportunity to experience love and joy. Perhaps that is the real lesson.

The story of the Garden of Eden offers an accurate symbolic picture of living in bliss and how bliss may not always be the choice we make. Many people infer that peace, flow, and bliss do not present the excitement and drama they seek. Bliss may even appear boring. They choose, instead, to add a bit of chaos to the mix. You know, stir the pot. They don't realize that drama and chaos often leave behind destruction.

So, back to the Garden of Eden and the high vibrational existence it typifies. We are supplied all things: food, shelter safety, love. Perhaps, we let our curiosity run away with us and, even though we are well supplied, we decide to taste forbidden fruit.

This quest (or fruit) may be borne of the desire for adventure, newness, perhaps even expansion. But the particular fruit (experience) we reach for is not available to us because it is reserved for our Source. This means that, this energy or portion of the garden, or inner self, is reserved as our way of giving back (returning energy to our Source). It means we are to live in gratitude, abundance and service to others. It is a symbol of the cycle of receiving and giving back and, thus, it is sacred.

Nevertheless, we eat the forbidden apple or quench our curiosity in ways that outlie our boundaries. And because we have intruded into sacred territory, we discover shame and quilt and, thus, lower our vibrational energy. And because we don't want to bear the brunt of our shame (breaking the rules), we blame the snake. *The serpent made us do it.* Hence, we continue to lower our energy and move from our Light body of bliss to a body of flesh and a mind of judgment.

Was this a mistake or a learning experience? In our quizzical state, were we looking to discover opposites? Right/wrong, up/down, hot/cold and judgment would certainly point out opposites.

It is true that we can discover these things and not judge them. Yet, the second we judge good or bad, we become trapped in the dense world. The analytical reasoning mind has taken over. We have lost our lightness and flow and made density real.

A Course in Miracles states that we got trapped in the idea of separation when we forgot to laugh. Instead of remaining in our intuitive mind of lightness and see the folly of our adventure, we forgot to laugh at the absurdity and, all of a sudden, the dense world of materiality seemingly became real. Perhaps important and measured. We took it all seriously and got trapped through the senses. It is the same way that someone forgets to laugh when insulted and becomes part of the drama. We forgot to laugh, and we lost (symbolically at least) our connection with our Source. In effect, we opened Pandora's box. It could have been an interesting story or adventure, but we took it too far. In our delusive mind, we took it seriously. Then the whole descent into matter.

Now, it is time to go back and see the truth. We are still divine beings. We continue to be the Light, and now we can observe the scene dispassionately and remember that it is a play to be enjoyed. It has the meaning we give it and no other.

Can we return to the Garden of Eden? Yes, let go of the angst that captures your attention and makes situations, events, opinions, and people you disagree with important, and return to your heart, where all of that is an illusion to play with, to learn from, and to enjoy. In other words, there is nothing to get worked up about.

You can't pay the bill on time. Pay what you can and contact the vendor. Accept what is and do your best. Tomorrow, there will be other possibilities.

A relationship ends. Be grateful for the time you had together and let go.

Someone is sick. Minister to them and love them. It is their journey.

You got the job, or you didn't get it. There is no insufficiency or lack. There is another one around the corner. Disconnect from the good-bad drama.

Someone is gay; someone is straight. Someone judges you. It has nothing to do with you. Be you. Do your best. No drama.

So, the journey takes us back to the heart (soul). The heart is our pathway to the soul. The soul is our connection to infinity (God). We learn how to live from our heart. It is the way to mastership.

You feel your way through life and that does not infer letting emotions rule the day. It does mean to go deep into your heart resonance and connect with your deepest essence. That is what differentiates what is right for you and what is not, what action, words, or study to initiate, how to expand and what it is that decreases you. We listen deeply with our feelings and are provided the truth. That is how we are to return to our inner garden and reconnect to bliss.

Come into the Kingdom as a Child - Wonderment

The Spiritual life does not remove us from the world
but leads us deeper into it.
Henri J M Nouwen

We are instructed in Matthew 18:3 *to enter the kingdom of Heaven as a child,* innocent, open, willing, vulnerable, without judgment. Can we do that?

Wonder is a newborn baby, wide-eyed when facing the adventure of earth. Just think of it: every color, shape, face is a moment of wonder. The baby does not presume to know what any of it means as he is taken with the charm and delight of each form. Can you look at the world in that way? Would you be willing to try?

Baby: *I don't know the meaning of any of it but it is amazing, and I can't wait to feel it, taste it, squish it.* The baby sees everything without preconception or judgment, which epitomizes openness and allows all possibilities and endless learning.

Judgments and squeezing things into small meanings block perception. The truth really is that we don't know the meaning of anything because the Universe has its own meaning and the ego has another one, and we are often programmed to accept the ego's interpretation. We aren't privy to the greater meaning until we drop (dissolve) the meaning the ego has assigned.

Letting the ego assign meaning keeps you small and often leads to blame, shame, bad and good, and all kinds of pronouncements. Then you fuss over to which category everything belongs. Is it necessary to belong to any category? The ego says yes and works hard to put and keep you there. You are a winner or loser. You are good or bad. You are an ethnic group and a political party and a religious denomination. You have a country and a history and lots of stories that relay who you are. All these categories restrict your energy and choices. The baby has none of that. He is joy-filled and amused because he is free. No judgment. Just fascination.

How do you recapture wonder? Let go of ego concerns that determine you must be right, wear the appropriate outfit, speak particular words, eat certain foods, know the right people, have a certain amount of money, be deemed "good," "a winner," "successful." None of it means anything. You can wear these badges and still not know God, or you can cultivate openness and willingness and be ready for anything. As a child, you can flow with Spirit and Spirit will be your guide and you'll end up right where you need to be.

Activity: Every day, go outside in nature or someplace different and be willing to look with wonder: How a leaf is made. The vibrancy of a color. The way one road flows into the next one. The roughness of tree bark. The taste of bread, etc. No judgment. Just wonderment.

Innocence

Youth is happy because it has the ability to see beauty.
Anyone who keeps the ability to see beauty never grows old.
Franz Kafka

Innocence: we had it in the beginning and then what happened? A child is born and no matter what color, shape, ethnic group, or tribe, it is beautiful. May we all wish to live in the purity and unbridled innocence of an infant. These brand-new beings exude perfection and love. It is all they know.

People are drawn to babies because they experience them as pure, open, without prejudice and willingness to accept.

Yes, this is true that, even though babies are without knowledge and don't know how to communicate beyond mumbled sounds and screeches and are incapable of controlling their body functions, they are beautiful, radiant beings. And even though they can't walk or talk, and they slobber their food, they are God's purest gift. They beam with love and possibility. That is the truth of who we are as well.

Babies are open to discovery. Thus, when Jesus said, *Come into the kingdom as a child,* you were given a major key to connecting to your innate state of Godliness or highest energy. Be innocent and open.

Babies represent a clean slate. There is no hate, anger, guilt or remorse marring their consciousness. Their focus is on awe and wonderment. A leaf can be an amazing item of texture, color, and even taste. Babies are interested. They want to experience everything through every sense. They have no judgment or pre-conception on good or bad. Everything is accepted in turn. What resides inside the waste can, or what amazing object sits on the top shelf of the bookcase, is open for discovery. Everything represents adventures to be had. Openness and innocence. That is the consciousness that Jesus referred to when he said to come into the kingdom as a child.

Come into the kingdom with innocence. Be witness to the wonderment of your true essence. Leave behind your illusions of negative judgments: guilt, shame, and wrongness. Keep your slate clean.

When you go to the movies, you are in observer-mode. You know that you are watching a made-up story, played out with actors that are assuming individual roles. You may enjoy the story, walk from the theatre, and within a few hours, you release the experience.

What if you adopted the same process with your earthly experiences? You know, the ones you feel have tainted you or made you unworthy, ignorant, or undesirable? What if you decide to look at those with wonderment and accept them as an earth movie in which each person was playing a part? Did you enjoy your role? Would you like to play a different character? What can you learn from the storyline? Have you played this part before? Is there a recurring theme? How do you want to change your character/role?

These are the questions we ask ourselves as we release the heaviness of an experience and move toward its greater meaning and purpose. The experience itself does not define you. It is just a part in the drama called life that you are acting out. It illustrates what you have magnetized and accepted in your consciousness. When you step back from the situation, you can see it more clearly. Once you recognize that you are not to be defined by a story or event, you are back in the theatre watching a new movie. You are "seeing" with objectivity, discernment and detachment. Perhaps even amusement.

Vulnerability as Strength

The two most important days in your life
are the day you were born and the day you find out why.
Mark Twain

Many people fear vulnerability. They will lie and make up stories to pretend that they are something they are not because they do not want to be seen as vulnerable. They hide lack of experience or knowledge for fear they may appear less important or valuable. They see vulnerability as weakness, a flaw, rather than strength, and that is an incorrect assumption and an illusion. Vulnerability is strength.

You might consider birds as small, vulnerable creatures. They are certainly tiny in size, but birds have tremendous staying power since they have been around for thousands of years. They must be doing something right.

The amazing quality that birds possess, along with other animals, is instinct or intuition. Whereas they have not been schooled in navigation or seasonal patterns, they nevertheless know the perfect time to fly south for the winter, how to build a nest, and how to prepare for and nurture a family. Many birds fly hundreds of miles with absolute trust, using seemingly tiny, frail wings, guided by an internal navigational system and, without error, land in the exact location they had intended. They do this by being vulnerable and willing to be guided by inner knowing.

Vulnerability, as described by Webster, is *openness*. Being open is a strength. It is the way we are led to new friends and experiences. Without openness, we are operating on a gerbil wheel, doing the same things, getting the same results, being bored and boring. But when we open ourselves to newness, the potential for aliveness is increased. That means going to an event where you know no one and start introducing yourself to strangers. That means taking a chance and applying for a job that might be above your skill level. And it means trying new things. Take dance lessons or a painting class or learn a new language. Be willing to be awful because you just might find out that you are a natural.

Here is a test:

What was the last thing you tried or attended when you were totally unprepared?

In that experience, what did you learn and how did you expand yourself?

What new experience can you sign on to right now?

Where have you wanted to travel and haven't yet given yourself permission?

What hobby might be fun to try? Chess, decorating, surfboarding, fishing, collecting, rehabbing, traveling, investing, learning calligraphy? Keep going. Pick one and give it a go without concerning yourself with excellence.

Practice being vulnerable (open), and you might discover strength you never knew you had.

Identification and Labels

God will not look you over for medals,
degrees or diplomas, but for scars.
Elbert Hubbard

From time immemorial, man has searched for meaning. We have searched because, initially, we formed a false sense of identity and found it unsatisfactory and inconclusive. It did not offer enough substance or meaning, so we searched.

In the beginning, as babies, we radiated love. When we beheld the world and the people around us, we were enthralled. At that time, we were still aware of our inner Source of love, and that made it possible to gaze at the material world without attachment. We viewed it with the eyes of wonder and fascination. We found amazement in everything: color, shapes, and forms. There was no judgment as to what was good and what was bad. We drank it in with relish and awe. It was fun!

Then something happened. Over time, we were informed that we were to be identified as Johnny, Suzi, Mary, or whoever. We were also told that we were *good* boys or girls or *bad* boys or girls, depending on someone else's opinion and needs. We began to fall into these descriptions and they shaped our ideas about ourselves. We formulated our personality and behavior accordingly. Survival required that we live within the parameters of *good,* so we learned to play that game. Because it seemed that survival was necessary and important, we focused our attention externally and, in the process, we forgot our spiritual core. We lost sight of the Light!

Soon, there was a material identity: a body, a toy, an opinion, a set of circumstances. My room, my bed, my toy, my mom, my ethnic group, etc. We were even educated and cultivated on what to believe, what the correct precepts were, who we were to like or disdain, and what God is. Day by day, we accepted this program and developed a sense of self. We formulated limitation and restriction, and no longer believed in our vastness or that we could move mountains.

With each presumption, life became serious and heavy and that was our error.

A Course in Miracles puts it this way. *"We forgot to laugh."* We may even have forgotten that we are always unconditionally and profoundly loved, and our internal Light is ever brilliant, no matter what.

Survival, being confirmed *good,* translated to being acceptable. Thus, our youthful open perception and willingness to enter life as an adventure evaporated, and our views about shape, color, size, intelligence, and worthiness restructured.

In turning our attention to the material world, our values changed and we believed that our source for love was the people around us: parents, siblings, peers, friends, employers, and so forth. The idea of proving our worthiness was born. Our security, indeed, our survival, teetered on this.

If something were to alter, like death, divorce, changing locations, performance at school, our security was challenged. It might even crumble. *Where is my toy, my friend, my room?* Soon, we were hooked in the material world, completely distracted from our Inner Light, our eternal Source of love and joy. That which initially made us complete, seemed to disappear. It no longer registered in our awareness.

The thing we did not know is that security can only be found in the internal world of Spirit, as the external world is constantly changing. Therefore, it is never stable or secure.

Thus, we adjusted our focus and made material accomplishments a lofty goal. *If I have the right education, make more money, own a bigger house, drive a faster car, then I will feel worthy and more secure.* The incessant race after things produced restlessness and lack of fulfillment because, no matter what, it would never be enough. We would never be secure.

The happiness that followed each shiny object was short-lived, only to be replaced with another quest. By this time, we were *stuck* in the sensory, material world and our self-worth became dependent on the grades we received, the brand of clothes we wore, the roles we played, our popularity, whether or not we were pretty or thin enough, and if we were associated with the right tribe. We lost our way. We became sidetracked and distracted from our center, our connection with the Universe, our inner Light.

A consciousness that is conditioned to identify with form (the physical body, job or career, quality of education, things that are owned) will find awareness of inner space nearly impossible.

This means, our ability to reconnect with our True Self has to be re-developed. Reconnection requires mental stability (focus) because the world of things is ever-guiding us away from the Light. Even when we attempt to provide self-loving attention, the focus ends up being on the physical form, such as exercise, eating nutritiously, facials, and massages, to name a few pampering activities, or to improve appearance and bodily well-being. In working from the sensory (material) realm primarily, we are still denying ourselves inner peace. We are mindful of thoughts about ourselves, but we are not *aware* of ourselves.

Our Greater Self (the Universe) wants the best for each person. It has *no* prejudices or biases. From that point of view, it doesn't even register ego identification. If you saw a child dressed up as a witch or a princess, you would know that she was playing with that identity. You would not be fooled into thinking that she is anything but a beautiful, glowing child underneath the garb. In the same way, God doesn't register your ego demeanor. God perceives his beautiful child in a glowing gown of Light. In the mind of God, you are the offspring, a bright light in the Universe.

You are a cell in the body of the Universe. You receive equal nourishment, joy, abundance, and grace as all other cells/beings. Only you, with a closed mind, can restrict this flow.

So, set your goals and trust that the Universe will help you to achieve them. To be effective in practicing the principle of non-attachment, you must believe that the Universe is abundant. No matter what you desire, it is available and on its way to you. Through the law of magnetic attraction, what you focus on increases.

Keep your focus clear, and allow the Greater Intelligence of the Universe to do its work. Everything is moving into the right place and time to bring you what you want or something even better.

Changing Your Emotional Identification

God is all reality, but not all reality is God.
Moses Cordovero

People often identify themselves by their emotions. Angry people have a hard time believing they can be peaceful. Depressed people identify with sadness and spend little or no time remembering happy moments. Instead, they take pills to adjust their neurology. Consequently, the same repeated memories keep them trapped.

To shift to a new paradigm may seem daunting, but it can be done and is accomplished all the time. It starts with training. What are you willing to dream? Can you dream a new reality and become impassioned by it?

Just as I used candle concentration exercises to develop strong concentration skills, you can do an identical process to adjust your emotional, magnetic resonance. You hold your attention on what you want and *feel* it. You keep your mind focused and, in so doing, lay down the tracks for future life experiences. This practice has to be repeated until it becomes your natural, default way of thinking. You are creating new neural pathways. It is the same as pulling up weeds. To keep the cleared space clean, you must plant new seeds, new behaviors. The seeds eventually take hold and get strong, and you become a new person with a new reality. The reality you want!

Then Came Roles

The soul is placed in the body like a rough diamond and must be polished, or the luster of it will never appear.
Daniel Defoe

Identity, on the surface, may seem complicated, but it really isn't.

The question is: With what do you identify? Many would say that they are English, Scottish, African-American, an executive, housewife, engineer, parent, or member of a particular political party. These descriptive terms differentiate according to roles you play in life, and they are all externally based because most folks look outside themselves for identity. This delineation could even include size or shape: I am tall, big-boned, handsome, redheaded, etc. These descriptions are body-oriented, therefore external. They define a condition (physical or philosophical) and a body type. They say nothing of the thinking-feeling inner being that expresses and creates through the body.

They are labels. Subterfuge. You might call them clues as to the role you are to play in this schoolroom called earth life. They do not reference your essential self. These external definitions are often the roadblocks in self-perception that we are to heal (correct).

To truly understand the subject of identity, you must look back at the process of evolution. In this particular life, being born was the beginning. But you go back well beyond that. Pay attention and you will discover the path.

People come into earth life ready to play a role. Each role helps you understand what you have learned thus far and what you have not. Each experience can lead to curiosity and discovery or shame and guilt. Your choice! Nevertheless, keep asking questions. *What else can I learn and do?*

In other words, you are *not* stuck in this movie, playing the same character, unless that is what you want. The vistas are wide open. What part would you like to play next? How can you land that role and perfect it? Choose: You can play the victim or the hero, the mentor or the student (or both), the parent or the child, the businessman or janitor, the queen or the pauper. So many roles. You will play many in your life. Have fun and learn from each of them. Remember they are roles, not you!

You did not start out in life with the concept that, if someone disapproves, it means something about you. Disapproval is about the person that is disapproving and no one else. When a person takes censure personally, it means they are having a hard time approving of themselves. Otherwise, it would not matter one way or another what someone else thinks about you.

The key to understanding this truth is realizing that YOU and only you are responsible for your own self-definition. You can see yourself as a magnificent God-Being with unlimited potential, or you can allow others to tell you who you are by relating to their small world of conclusions. It is your ultimate choice.

Albert Einstein was judged an idiot when he was a child. The problem is that he had lived in a higher consciousness than most and did not learn the way others learned. (This is true of many today, as well.) His conceptual mind sought to dream and ponder. The truth is that he was not designed to be "normal" and, for some wonderful reason, he didn't attempt to confine himself within those tiny borders. Because he knew that imagination leads the way, he indulged his imagination and let it take him to major discoveries in the field of science and, specifically, quantum physics.

The same thing is true of Thomas Edison, the master inventor, who was judged unteachable, basically an idiot. His mother did not buy this analysis and decided to teach him herself. The result was a person with a genius mentality that was the innovator of his age, with over 200 registered inventions to make life on earth easier and communication across continents possible.

Many found Edison's deafness an untenable handicap, a problem. He considered deafness an asset in that he did not have to partake in mundane, nonsensical conversations. He also did not take on the opinions of others who lacked the imagination and inspiration to develop the Dictaphone, phonograph, incandescent light bulb, earliest motion picture cameras, and hundreds of other inventions that expanded everyone's experience. He understood his gift and was committed to using it.

Dissolving the Ego

Awakening is not changing who you are
but discarding who you are not.
Deepak Chopra

A Course in Miracles, a spiritual study of self-reconciling dictated through psychologist Helen Schucman, indicates that to dissolve the ego (external) identity, we must return to the innocence of a child and let go of preconceived ideas and judgments as they have narrowed our potential, vision and capabilities. Identification with externals, like religions, politics, ethnic or social groups, etc., narrows self-perception and possibilities. With this insistent outer focus, we become small and separate from our inner Light. We lose the magnificence and potential of the pure God (Spirit) energy that we are. We narrow ourselves, placing ourselves outside the vast field of potentiality.

Example: If I were to define myself as a mathematician or scientist, does that mean I am not an artist or inventor? Or, if my belief is that I can't do something, does that mean this limitation is real? Can we not claim all things as our total makeup?

As we return to *A Course in Miracles,* there is a passage that states, *I don't know the meaning of this…chair or that flower or that television or book.* What this exercise and declaration does is bring us back into the unsullied openness of a child who looks at life in wonderment. A child gazes at the world with wide-open awe, without preconception, prejudice or judgment. A child will ignore his toys and play with a box or bread-twister, finding each item fascinating. A child's world is full of exciting places and things to explore. From the guileless mind of a child, there is not one person better or worse than another, for he accepts them all equally. This is what consciousness without ego is like and an example of living in the vastness of Spirit.

Dissolving the ego is necessary to fully experience spiritual life, energy, and potential for this is when you know that anything is possible. It is when you understand that the only limitations that exist are the ones you imagine and invent.

The question, then, is how to return to this guileless state? This is followed by another: Are you willing to drop your good-bad judgments and allow everything an equal value?

How do we do this? What is the process?

A Course in Miracles suggests you start each day with the notion that *I don't know the meaning of this situation, relationship, item or form.* This simple statement allows you openness and returns your attention to the innocence of a child that does not pretend to assign rigid meanings. In this way, you dissolve the ego's need to run the show and to have all the answers. From there, you can live in freedom in the vast possibility of the Universe.

Activity: Start each day with *I don't know the meaning of today. I am wide open to be guided by Spirit.*

How to Practice Innocence Now

The moment one gives close attention to anything,
even a blade of grass, it becomes a mysterious, awesome,
indescribably magnificent world in itself.
Henry Miller

This practice requires patience and discipline. These are divine soul qualities that everyone possesses. It is a matter of giving full attention to your desire for highest connection and experience that motivates you to practice innocence.

Keep a journal as this practice will establish mindfulness. Record, on a daily basis, observations of people and events. For instance, when you meet a person, record your observations and ask yourself if these observations are judgmental or objective. For instance, if you see your neighbor, do you feel open and friendly? Or avoidance? Or judgment, based on appearance or behavior? Do you *observe* or *judge*? How would a baby experience your neighbor?

Use the same exercise for an event, meeting, or interaction. What do you feel? What do you observe? What can you find in this experience that is awe-inspiring?

Spend time in nature daily and notice colors, textures, and shading. Hold a leaf and feel its texture, size, shape, and smell: its essence. Notice the air. What does it feel like as it brushes your skin or lifts your hair? What textures, smells, and shapes can you observe and experience? How can you let your senses expand in a state of wonderment?

Chapter 2: Light

You Are the Light of the World

I AM the Light of the World – YOU are the Light of the World.
Matthew 5:14

There are many near-death experiences reported wherein an individual describes a beautiful, warm, loving Light that engulfs the whole being. At contact with this nurturing, healing Light, all concern, worry, and discomfort disappears and makes way for the comfort and ease of unconditional love. In this experience, the individual is baptized with the cleansing properties of love.

An interesting fact about this Light experience is that it is always with us and available. We don't have to wait for death to experience it. This cosmic Light is the all-encompassing element in which we live. We can find it within.

We have been trained to think of ourselves as human beings as opposed to spiritual beings, and we have been indoctrinated with the idea of limitation. In other words, because the body vehicle is relatively small and limited (requiring food, water, sleep, housing) as we identify with it, we believe that we are also limited. Yet, as you realize the body is a temporary vehicle in much the same way as an automobile is a temporary vehicle that gets you from here to there, while the soul or spirit is a forever vehicle (the rider in the car), you can adjust your view to identify as the Greater Self (Spirit/Soul), thus releasing the concept of material limitation that has been learned and adopted. For instance, the edict, *I Am the Light of the World* places you in the internal realm of Spiritual Light as your true form and identification.

The question is: How do you release the dense body as your focal point of identification, so you may assume the truth of who you really are as the Light Energy of your Eternal Being? And thus, you may assume a vaster vehicle and identity.

To do this, begin by distinguishing the mental architecture (beliefs and stories) you have constructed and accepted. Through this imaginary structure, you have contrived a life of difficulty and struggle. Here is an example of imagined beliefs: *You must work hard to get ahead; the body is frail and victim to disease and viruses; other people have power over you.* These mental concepts have been indoctrinated, taught, repeated, and accepted. They are only truth when you adopt them. For those who have adopted a broader view, larger possibilities exist.

Genesis, Chapter 1: First story of creation: *In the beginning, when God (Universal Intelligence) created the heavens and the earth, the earth was a formless wasteland and darkness covered the abyss, while a mighty mind (thought) swept over the waters (substance). Then God said, "Let there be light," and there was light.* The Quantum Field of Energy was thus brought into creation.

Quantum physicists assert that the Universe is a quantum field of energy (Light) and that everything that exists, exists within this field. Thus, you exist within this field as well. This field (or body of Light energy) that you really are, is all-powerful and limitless and accepts whatever program (idea) you give it. It is comparable to a computer that accepts whatever software program you install in it. That means that you also have the power to delete programs, edit programs, and create new programs. (The original concept of the computer was based on, or mirrored, the structure of the mind.) Each person, as a Divine Light Being, also morphs into whatever the mind sets as its program. This gives you immense power to change, become, and expand, i.e., *Change Your Thinking; Change Your Life* (by Ernest Holmes).

Because you have spent many years repeating the program, *I am powerless, helpless, sick, weak, and struggling,* instead of *I AM the beauty and Light of the world; I AM powerful, omniscient, and without limit,* you must now edit and install new software (beliefs and stories).

What would happen if you addressed every situation with the mental construct of vastness, mutability, and power? *I Am the Light of the world. All power is mine and every possibility is available to me. I Am open to experience the highest intelligence, possibility, and solutions.* Try it and find out.

If you are determined to create a new expanded program, you would eventually, perhaps sooner rather than later, open to a new you. You would begin to live more in the Light than in the dense expression of materiality. You would see yourself as a Divine Being rather than a small body operating in the world of time and space.

Does this scare you? Does it excite you? Check your reaction to these ideas. Your reaction determines your readiness. A faint heart yields a weak result. You decide what will be.

I Am the Light of the world will call your Light Spiritual Beingness to your awareness. You can frame this new self as *I Am the Light; I Am the inner essence of Spirit. I vibrate in joyful connection to Spirit. I Am Spirit.* Adjust the affirmation according to your understanding.

When Jesus said, *I AM the Light of the world,* he also said, *YOU are the Light of the world.* He was speaking of establishing your sense of identity to the truth of your being.

We are all Light conceived. The dense body proceeds or projects from that inner essence of creation. We can place our focus at either place and that focus determines our destiny.

Are you ready to release the heaviness of the mental constructs you took on as a child? If so, you have a new way ahead. Begin the process. State daily: *I Am the Light of the world. All possibilities are open to me. The egoic self no longer controls with its smallness. I open to my Greater Self and every possibility. I AM the Light.* With each day of practice your identification with your limitless potential expands.

By the way, Light and Love is the same thing, which is to say that you are the Love of the world, too.

The Expansive Universe

The Holy Land is everywhere.
Black Elk, Native American

Quantum physicists tell us that the Universe is always expanding. We are to match the Universe. Self-mastery denotes expansion. The desire to expand in wisdom and practice is natural and aligned with our Divinity. We are in and of this ever-expanding Universe, and that means there is an urge within each person to expand with it. It means that we are to expand beyond the self that came into this world. As we grow, understand more, and apply the truth, we become more. We expand. We learn to live in sync with our essential or true selves. This is why people like Orville and Wilbur Wright, Thomas Alva Edison, Bill Gates, and Steve Jobs were driven to bring invention to the world. As they engaged their imaginations and technical skills, they brought brilliance to the world in the form of invention, mechanics, and technology. They blessed everyone because they paid heed to inspiration. They went with it. Each of us has the same brilliance and resourcefulness. We are to find that to which we resonate to. What field of invention, creativity, resourcefulness, imagination, or endeavor is ours to explore? It is the gift we came into life to develop and share.

If we were to drop the external pursuit of quotas, competition, and comparisons, we would be left with the spirit of freedom that urges us to peek into the next challenge and find a place for our curiosity of what works and what doesn't. By opening our minds to potentials and *allowing*, Spirit responds, and we are delivered insight, vision, and even steps to utilize magic into our endeavors. We were born with this energy, a limitless imagination of possibilities that can take form as we give it life.

Academy award-winning actress, Jane Fonda, spoke about finding her dream, *My problem was not knowing what my dream was. Once I knew what my dream was, I could afford to follow it.* And when Fonda discovered her passion, she threw herself into it, and the result was acclaim and fulfillment. Thus, it is with everyone.

Activity: Each night before you go to bed, write a letter to Spirit. It will be something like this.

Dear Spirit: I am so grateful that you are my guide. I ask that you guide me to recognize what my divine purpose and work is to be. I commit to listening to all the cues and signs and willingly follow up in whatever way I am directed. I commit to listening without judgment as the ideas flow to me, and I commit to taking action with each inspiration. I am your loving partner.

Then, sign the letter.

Put it aside and go to sleep. The next day, pay attention to the cues and signs as they appear and follow up in whatever way seems appropriate. Next night, do the same thing. Keep a log along with your letter, and you will begin to see a pattern emerge. Follow it.

Everything Is Energy

Our deepest fear is not that we are inadequate.
Our deepest fear is that we are powerful beyond measure.
Marianne Williamson

From a drop of water to a massive oak tree, everything is comprised of energy. This chapter provides a way to develop the mental discipline needed to direct your energy toward the objectives you desire.

Through his research, Albert Einstein tells us that everything in our world is energy. There are two kinds of energy: manifest energy, which we see in the form of books, furniture, cars and physical bodies, and unmanifest energy, which is everything else, including thought. Manifest energy vibrates slowly enough to be seen with the dull instruments of the eyes. It is easy to identify with manifest energy and forms because, most of the time, we are looking to the world and identifying with our physical form. In other words, we see ourselves as a body.

Yet, everything else in the Universe is also energy. This includes our thoughts and feelings. It is easy to recognize energy when you think in logical terms. For instance, if you were to walk into a room where everyone is laughing and having fun, you would feel happy energy. By the same token, if you enter a room where people are miserable, sad, disheartened, you feel "down" or depressed energy. If you entered a room where everyone was talking about you, you would feel that energy as well. It might appear in your awareness as discomfort or resistance.

There is a magnetic quality to energy. For instance, if you are a happy, up-beat person, you tend to feel most comfortable around other positive folks. Contrarily, if you tend to whine and complain, you connect best with woe-is-me types. You know, negative folks. It is all a matter of energy. You feel most comfortable around energy that matches your own. If you have ever felt that you were at the wrong place with the wrong people, then you know what I mean.

We have free will. We can choose our thoughts, our position, and our outlook. We can seek out negatives or positives and, in so doing, we create or tailor our lives and energy. We actually set ourselves up for the experiences and people we draw (magnetize) into our lives.

Thoughts and experiences have a cause-effect relationship. We hold an intention and we magnetize or draw to us the circumstances that fulfill that intention. For instance, if you are wanting more friends, you might begin to notice opportunities to join clubs, or you take note of interesting classes where you can meet people, or networking events, or you might pay attention to party invitations that you had previously ignored. All of this is synchronistic with the intention of having more friends.

The same thing is true if you want a new job, better health, or if you feel trapped. You energize thoughts of being trapped and continue to magnetize situations where you feel trapped. Remember, of course, that if there is a trap, there is a door out of the trap. Not everyone is willing to open the door.

Again, bitter people attract situations where they can continue feeling bitter, and optimists magnetize opportunity and advantage. It is a matter of choice and the way we condition ourselves.

The odds were against J. K. Rowling, the author of the *Harry Potter* books. She was a single mother on public assistance when she wrote her first best-selling book. Throughout she held her vision on a career as a successful writer and since then, she has been on the best-selling book list many times.

And the odds were against weigh-loss expert Richard Simmons. Simmons' private struggle with obesity generated a determined focus. He wanted to help other overweight people to lose weight and regain their health, confidence and self-esteem. His perseverance led to a successful business that included videotaped aerobic classes and a deal-a-meal program. He brought his dream to reality and assisted millions to lose weight and get fit.

What kind of energy are you creating in your life? Are you choosing to view the world as filled with potential, or do you see darkness, negativity, lack and limitation? Discipline to manage your mind is a necessary requirement to get you where you want to go. Master your mind as a directing beam and stay focused, no matter what. Rowlings did and Simmons did, and so can you.

Your mind is a filter and what you think, you choose. Are you happy with your choices, or is it time to refocus and shape your energy (and life) in a more appropriate, expansive way?

Energy Must Be Expressed

No man becomes rich unless he enriches others.
Andrew Carnegie

It is true that energy must be expressed. Repressing energy is like sitting on a volcano that is ready to erupt. It will erupt. Observe people who repress their natural instincts and you will be watching a bomb ready to go off. Without direction and purpose, destruction takes place. Observe a child during a tantrum and you will see spastic energy being thrown off to relieve inner pressure (an inner volcano erupting).

There is a fundamental principle about energy: It cannot remain static. It has to express, move. Movement is the nature of energy. You can't set it down like a coffee cup. It will not remain there. It has to move because it is life.

If there is no downward movement (activity expression in the dense, material world), the only option is to move/express upward. That means it can move into or hit the higher mind (superconscious), at which point the energy sensation is that of a spiritual orgasm. In fact, the sensation of a physical, sexual orgasm pales in comparison. It is not a quantitative difference because a spiritual orgasm is thousands of times greater in quantity. It is a quality difference. Whereas a sexual organism is momentary, a spiritual orgasm goes beyond the moment and evokes change that lasts forever.

As energy touches your highest consciousness, you are showered with joy. This internal shift arouses your intuitive function. Intuition is a subtle energy. It is the subtlest thing in you. Just as you allow your instinct to exist, you allow and give total freedom to your intuition to be fulfilled. And as you do, you will be surprised at the kinds of powers you have been carrying within you.

When you eliminate repression from your consciousness, your instinct has a different quality to it. It is joined with intelligence. It now becomes your greatest resource in living a life of freedom, creativity, and movement. (More on intuition in Chapter 5.)

To recognize the energy you were designed to express, pay attention to the activities you love doing. Most of these are activities that come naturally to you, like playing with children, writing poetry, building a structure, programming a computer, rebuilding an engine, decorating a room, performing a role on stage. There are endless ways to express energy. Or you could get quiet and ask for guidance. *What is my unique way of expressing energy?* The answer I received was *Teach.* And, yes, I have been teaching my whole life.

People as Globes of Energy

> *People tell you the world looks a certain way. Parents tell you how to think. Schools tell you how to think. TV. Religion. And then at a certain point, if you're lucky, you realize you can make up your own mind. Nobody sets the rules but you. You can design your own life.*
>
> Carrie Ann Moss

Often, we see people as physical bodies and when we do, we underestimate who they are because a body symbolizes limitation. Yet, we can still observe them in a more truthful manner. If we were to view people as globes of energy, we would begin to see vaster potential. The more we understand each person as a complex expression of energy patterns, we can begin to comprehend cause and effect.

Someone is alcoholic for a reason beyond the addiction. Another person has diabetes beyond the fact that the person doesn't care about health. There are deeper issues that evoke the way energy moves in our lives.

Example: A young man who had power in past lives and had abused it, cannot go forward until there is rebalancing. If he had been abusive to people who could not protect themselves, in his present experience, he is placed in a position to be abused. It is not punishment; it is rebalancing. He must *see* (experience) what he had done and be willing to make amends. This is necessary because he has power and ability and must find a correct way to use it.

By going through difficult experiences, this man has the opportunity to observe life from different points of view. His wild, out-of-control ego is tempered and he is able to connect with a deeper sense of kindness within his soul. You might say his powerful energy has come full circle to assist him to be the person he was designed to be.

Another individual, a woman, may have practiced self-denial and self-abuse to the point of creating a condition of illness. This one has put her attention on receiving love from her children to the exclusion of giving herself love. In other words, she has not cultivated self-love or self-expression and put the onus of being loved externally. She has held on to her children in her own self-interest. She has lost her center and personal value because she sees herself as valueless, not loveable, not worth loving herself.

People with self-value cultivate their talents and self-expression. It is not about status or accruing money. It is about cultivating innate talents and abilities to contribute to a world they had entered to experience.

When we give of ourselves through talents, abilities, experiences, and expressions, we receive in turn. In fact, the more we give, the more we receive. That is how energy works. You cannot give with a pure intention without receiving. You will notice that I speak of *pure giving*: giving with intent. This excludes giving to look good, or to achieve status, or to impress others.

The Cause and Effect of Energy Expression

It is our mind that makes monsters out of moments.
Guy Finley

In our purest essence, we have much to give. It can be words of encouragement or wisdom, opportunities for others to share their talent, money to assist someone in need, or service to those who cannot do for themselves. There are many ways to give and all are important. Your particular gift is an extension of who you are, your personal expression, and that is what you are being asked to give.

Energy is always available in vast quantities. Consider the circular movement of energy. You speak truth to someone and the energy you expended projects out from you and circles back around and returns to you expanded. It works the same way when energy is misdirected or negative. When you are resentful or angry that energy projects out from you and returns in dire circumstances or negative energy patterns.

I know a woman who pocketed anger and resentment for years. She recently discovered that she had cancerous tumors in her body. These internal growths represent accumulations of toxic energy (anger) formulated as cancerous growths in her body. Just as anger is self-destructive, cancer, as a physical reflection, is the body's way of turning on itself. Yes, cancerous (unnatural growth) must be removed and healed in the same way that the internalized anger and resentment must be healed. Healing is accomplished on every level. You can't heal the outer, external body permanently without going to the core of the inharmonious thought pattern and healing it as well.

Healers have referenced the body as the unconscious mind and, as such, it reveals our beliefs, attitudes, how we choose to live, our discrepancies and errors. It does not lie. Thus, the most authentic thing you can do is to take responsibility for the body and that which it is expressing. That means care for it as a precious gift, for it is the vehicle you will use to express your divine energy throughout this lifetime. So, when your body is telling you that you are stressed or angry, believe it. Don't wait to offer solace when it is dis-eased or immobile. Listen now and rebalance in this moment.

Masculine and Feminine Energies: How They Work

The least of things with a meaning is worth more in life
than the greatest of things without it.
Carl Jung

In the material world, masculine qualities are used for functioning (being active) on a daily basis. These qualities include aggressiveness, action, directness, movement, dominance, motivation and drive.

On the other hand, feminine qualities (energy) are epitomized by receptivity, listening, intuition, sensitivity, patience, empathy, and nurturing. Feminine qualities are lighter and softer than masculine qualities and each serve their purpose. We need both.

To focus into the higher, lighter energy of Spirit, we must use our feminine qualities of listening, intuition, receptivity and nurturing. They set up the mindset necessary to connect with the subtle energy of Light.

Everyone possesses masculine and feminine attributes. We use them constantly in everyday situations. Both energies, masculine and feminine, have value in specific situations. If you want to get things done, you move into action and use masculine energy. If you want to connect with another person, you listen and become receptive to their needs, using feminine qualities. Each individual chooses the qualities that is to be expressed on whatever occasion arises. The point to note is that *it is a choice.*

Nurturing New Life

Heaven is a state of mind, not a location,
since Spirit is everywhere and in everything.
Wayne Dyer

Over my long career as a Transformational Coach, I have dealt with many women who desired to become pregnant and appeared unable to do so. To a person, these women operated in highly driven career positions that required concentration on getting things done, masculine energy. I instructed each one that, in order to become pregnant, she must learn to receive. In other words, move away from her masculine, aggressive mindset and enter the feminine energy of receptivity, stillness, and nurturing. She must become a willing receptacle for new life to develop. She must receive the sperm that will germinate into new life. When each woman shifted into a receptive state, she became pregnant. She received and nurtured the sperm that implanted her egg and that germinated into new life.

It is simple reasoning. To receive the sperm and be open to impregnation, there must be a state of openness, inviting, and allowing. Receiving is a state of inviting and allowing: feminine characteristics. While a woman was demonstrating masculine traits of pushing, driving, and aggressive action, her feminine nature and ability to conceive new life was curtailed.

The energy we express dictates everything: accomplishment, creativity, ability to listen internally and externally, health, abundance…everything! If you are always aggressive and never receptive, you will wear yourself out. If you are always receptive and never aggressive, you will not accomplish anything. The key is balance.

Do you need the answer or solution to a concern? If so, you want to focus intuitively or spiritually, and that requires stillness. Set aside time daily to be silent. You can do this by gazing out a window, walking in the woods, floating on a raft, gazing at the night sky. Each of these activities stills the mind. A quiet mind is receptive to inner guidance.

Chapter 3: Mastering the Mind - The Mind Is a Tool!

Step Back to Become the Observer

Curving back within myself, I create again and again.
The Bhagavad Gita

In the same way that you sit in a movie theatre and watch a movie on the silver screen, you learn to sit back and observe life. When you are taking in a movie, you know it is a movie. That doesn't mean you don't get involved and want the "good guys" to triumph. Yet, still, when you leave the theatre, the movie no longer exists. It is gone!

The same thing is true of earth life. You can laugh, enjoy, cry, lament, and experience every emotion, but it will still conclude and you will eventually walk out of the theatre of life. Hopefully, at that point, you are wiser, more loving and compassionate than you were when you took on your current role.

The more you learn to observe life situations rather than become attached to them, your chance of profound learning and growth are exponentially improved. Plus, you get to live a joyful life.

Willie Nelson, the great musician, songwriter, and guitar picker, is a great example of this principle of mindfulness. He started his career in the small town of Abbott, Texas, over eighty years ago. Along the way, he worked in small beer joints and cafes, then later in sports stadiums and magnificent venues. His songs were hits some of the time and, other times, not so much.

As a true cowboy, or highwayman, as he calls it, he followed the path he was on and, whether he was outdoors singing in the park or in a glorious concert hall, the one constant was love: God, music, family, and friends. When he had found out that his manager had not paid his taxes for three years, and he was facing bankruptcy and the ire of the IRS, he decided to get busy, play his music, pay the government, and let go of worry. Others suggested he give in to the government threat and go bankrupt. He said, “No.”

His consistent mindful focus on what he loved (music) kept him moving and, in his estimation, healthy. He knew that relationships came and went, some of his songs hit big and others did not, most people were trustworthy and some were not and, still, in the long run, he kept his center, stayed focused, and played music. No matter what happened, he went back to his center and trusted the flow that always provided the next song and opportunity.

As life required, Willie Nelson kept his mind focused in the present moment by letting go of impermanence (money, people, recording companies, associates, record deals, houses). Yet he always lived in a state of love.

In his case, he loved God, family, friends, and music. It was his way to observe the particulars of any situation and make his best move without gambling that it was his only move.

Nelson is one example. There are many others. People who detach from attachment to observe the moment they are in and trust the larger picture, are legionary: Thomas Edison, Abraham Lincoln, Mother Teresa, Nelson Mandela, Paramahansa Yogananda, the Yogi who opened the West to Yoga, to name a few.

Imagine that you are on a raft in the river, flowing gently, and you give permission to the river to take you, to hold you, and to guide you. This metaphor brings to mind your agreement to let the Universe take hold in your life and flow its energy through you. As you do this, you open a channel to greater creativity and you give up resistance. In other words, you trust that the Universe knows the way and you don’t, even if you think you do. Thus, the river takes you gently on your ride and you get to observe how your desire comes into fruition without judging or struggling but just acting appropriately as the occasion arises.

Life is an adventure at best, and you get to learn amazing lessons and build strength and character as you traverse through it. Hence, learning to step back in each new venue and ask, *What is the purpose of this?* helps you gain clarity, wisdom and stature. Plus, you keep stress and angst to a minimum.

Mindfulness - Listening Beyond the Noise

He is blessed over all mortals who loses no moment
of the passing life in remembering the past.
Henry David Thoreau

The discipline of learning to stay focused in the present moment is a great practice to achieving mastery and peace. Often, people spend their precious moments longing to be somewhere else or doing something else. Or they work from a pre-ordained plan and are ever-focused into the future. Or they waste time lodged in the past, remembering everything that happened and often re-living it. Or they worry, feel guilty and anxious about the future. The past and the future are not available. We can do nothing about them. But we have this precious present moment to live right now.

One of the ways we can practice being in the present is by becoming a *watcher* or *observer*. Every moment that we decide to observe our experience, we become unhooked from it. We become non-attached and non-reactive. By standing back and holding a bit of distance from the drama of the moment, we create reserves of energy that will help us perform right-action as events evolve.

Being in the moment as the observer is preparation for a deeper practice, like meditation. The whole idea of releasing our chattering mental monologues assists in achieving a more stable consciousness of peace.

In being anchored in the present, we become privy to the mental chatter that can take up all our mental space with possessive, addictive thoughts. By being present, we come to recognize that we have two voices within us.

The first one is the voice of truth. It comes to us subtly and offers suggestions: *Join that club. It's a good place to grow. You did a great job with that. Drive a new route to work today. Now is the time to call that customer. You are ready to move to a new house, job, state, relationship, etc. Study anthropology or journalism or whatever. Open your own business.*

This voice appears as light energy. Positive. When we follow the voice of truth, our lives are ever-changing and we are continually growing. This inner voice will lead us down a path and, in time, we will discover, with delight, the answers to our questions in addition to gaining the growth we need to progress to our desired outcome.

The second voice is the voice of doubt. It will tell us things like: *Don't join the club. You're not good enough to do that. Stay on the same tried and true path even though it goes nowhere. Change is scary. Don't call that customer; you'll be bothering him. Put it off. He won't buy anything anyway. Stay in the job. It's a sure thing. Keep your benefits – you need them. Stay in the house. Moving to a new neighborhood is scary, unpredictable.* This voice feels heavy and tends toward fear. Using Jerry Steinfeld's vernacular, this voice would be heard as, "Yada, yada, yada."

Whichever voice you choose to listen to will eventually get louder. It can even drown out the other one. You can tell which voice you are heeding by noticing the quality of your life. Are you living a life of joy, freedom, and expression? Or does your life reflect fear, restriction, resignation, and the eternal quest for safety? Do you venture out to discover and try new things, or do you avoid change? One way evokes joy and the other evokes fear.

One way to ascertain which voice you follow is by stepping back and observing. As you watch your thoughts, feelings, and behaviors, you begin to notice which voice you cultivate and which voice motivates you. Then, without recrimination or guilt, you can make corrections.

Love and Fear

Everyone is on a spiritual path; most people just don't know it.
The spiritual journey is the unlearning of fear and the acceptance of love.
Marianne Williamson

We are moved by two things, love and fear. Love comes from the voice of truth and fear emanates from the voice of ego. When people set out to do something, they proceed with one or the other voice urging them on. For example, I may stop and get my car fueled because I want to enjoy the freedom of going wherever I choose. A full gas tank affords me that freedom. Or, I may stop and fill my gas tank because I am *afraid* of running out of gas. The first statement reflects joy and expansion. The second reflects fear.

The voice of fear also shows itself in resistance. Many people resist moving forward. They may think that they are maintaining the status quo to stay right where they are. It seems comfortable. But are they really feeling comfort or is it stagnation?

The problem with attempting to stay put is that the Universe does not stop moving. There is constant movement and change. In fact, the only constant in life is change. As the Buddhists say, "Change is." When you resist life, you go against the flow.

Therefore, ask yourself, *Am I moving forward or resisting life?* Then decide, given your preferences, what is the best approach for you.

The author and teacher, Eckhart Tolle, described a time when he was deeply depressed. A thought came to him, *I don't think I can live with myself any longer*. That statement caught his attention, and he wondered if he was one person or two: the *I* and *myself*. *Who is this I? And who is myself?* This query began his process of waking up to become the observer of his thoughts.

Who is the "I" that cannot live with myself? By watching his thoughts, he came to realize that he had two minds: one of dissension and unhappiness, the ego, and another that observed and decided. He also found that, when he entered stillness, there was peace. This is how he cultivated the understanding that he needed to live in peace with himself. Through his writings and seminars, Tolle has instructed many others to do the same. You can find his teaching in his books: *The New Earth* and *The Power of Now.*

Activity: Your exercise in this chapter is to stand back and to become the *watcher.* Do this for at least four minutes four times every day. Observe your thoughts, feelings, and behaviors. Ask yourself: *With this decision, thought, or action, am I moving forward or resisting life?* The activities that follow will help you recognize which voice (love or fear) you are listening to.

Make a list of those things (activities, responsibilities, jobs, commitments, etc.) that you find yourself resisting. For example, *I resist keeping good tax records. I resist setting a day aside for relaxation and fun. I resist meditating. I resist eating healthy foods.*

Study each item. Is it for your highest good? Is it busy work, something you feel you *should* do but will not assist you in your growth? Mark these items as a "should" or as a "growth," something that would help you expand.

Address each item you have designated as being for your highest good. Examine each one and ask: *What do I find objectionable about this item?* Answer below, saving space for another entry to follow.

Item 1:

Item 2:

Item 3:

Item 4:

Regarding each item, consider: *How can I turn this objection around? How can I adjust my point of view and see it as something I want to do?* Make a note under each objection

Out of the above listed items, choose one that you are willing to change today. Create a plan to make this change. Write your plan here.

What to Do with Mental Chatter

They always say time changes things,
but you actually have to change them yourself.
Andy Warhol

Mental chatter is an indication of engrossment (entrapment) in matter or form. Most people make mental chatter their identification. That means the continuous flow of thoughts, i.e., worry, fretting, remembering, second-guessing, what to do next, etc., goes on incessantly while the individuals believe that it is who they are. It is much the same as believing their form or physicality is who they are. With external identification, there is no peace to be found, because the material world and the mental chatter that goes with it are ever-changing.

Neither the material world nor the mental chatter is representative of who you are. Only the peace that resides deep within your consciousness is who you are. The key is to learn how to live *in* the world but not be *of* the world.

Babies exude this consciousness of Light until they are taught otherwise. Babies radiate the Light to the world and they are happy. Perhaps it is time to rediscover that Light. Perhaps it is calling to you. With disciplined attention, you will find it again.

There is a story that illustrates what it takes to move into your inner depth of stillness. A Zen Master strolled along a mountain path with one of his students. On the path stood a lovely tree with spread-out branches just right for a picnic lunch. The master and student sat and ate their simple lunch.

The young student was eager to glean the wisdom of his master. He had not yet discovered the key to mastering the mind. Thus, he asked the question, "Master, how do I enter Zen?" (*How do I enter the state of consciousness known as Zen or stillness*?)

The Master was a patient, thoughtful persona. He hesitated for a few minutes while his student waited in anticipation. Finally, he spoke, "Do you hear the trickle of the mountain stream as it flows?

The student was so enamored with his busy mind-chatter that he had not noticed the music of the mountain stream. He focused his mind to hear the sound of the stream. Quieting his mind to listen to the sounds of nature was challenging. Finally, his mind quieted and his awareness heightened. He responded to his master, "Yes, I can hear it."

The Master instructed, "Enter Zen from there."

A little while later, the student was captured once again by his restless mind as he had lost the alert stillness of the previous moment. He queried once again, "Master, I am curious as to what you would have said, if I had not been able to hear the sound of the mountain stream?"

The Master thoughtfully considered this question and responded, "Enter Zen from there." Hence, the master indicated that, no matter where you are, you can achieve stillness from there. In fact, the stillness of Zen is always available, anytime, anywhere, to anyone willing to discipline the mind to enter.

Do you recognize the restless student, who was so preoccupied with questions, that he could not sit in silence? Many relate to this scenario as it suggests a metaphor for identifying the undisciplined mental state they inhabit daily. The undisciplined mind is continuously moving and focused on the external world. Thus, it lacks the ability to be quiet. This restless chatter robs you of peace. It is only through stilling the mind over and over that mental strength is achieved and one can enter Zen.

Moving into Zen is the same as returning to your inner state of peace. Mental discipline is required to do this. The technique called meditation can supply that. Meditation is a process by which you relax the body and conscious mind and move into inner silence (Zen/stillness). Instead of investing every waking moment to the endless mental chatter of the undisciplined mind, you can listen deeper and move into deeper space.

This practice brings heightened awareness and brings the opportunity to reestablish your inner connection with Spirit. Many people feel incapable of holding their attention on inner stillness because they give in to the ego's chaos. This random chatter arises from the mental program you were developed to experience as a human, rather than as a spiritual being.

Set an Intention and Do NOT Falter!

> *All power is within you; you can do anything and everything. Believe in that, do not believe that you are weak; do not believe that you are half-crazy lunatics, as most of us do nowadays. You can do anything and everything, without even the guidance of anyone. Stand up and express the divinity within you.*
>
> Swami Vivekananda

What do you *really* want? Can you believe in your desire? Can you stay focused? When you dance or perform other creative activities, you are in the here and now. You are feeling the moment while the mind wants to dash off and analyze and dream up worst-case scenarios. But when you set a firm intention and stay true to it, you can move mountains.

Consider how successful people think. They think beyond ordinary boundaries to perceive something extraordinary. Everyone has this capability. It requires your commitment to choose your thoughts.

Ordinary folks let circumstances control them. Extraordinary people transform their circumstances and find the pearl in each situation. This can be done no matter what your current role is in life. This is all about mind control. For instance, what might appear to be an ordinary job can be converted into a doorway or steppingstone to your dream-life, achieved through mind control.

Here are some examples of people who started their careers in an ordinary job by sorting mail and used it as a steppingstone to greater things.

Simon Cowell, the multi-millionaire music mogul of American Idol and The X Factor, started his career in the EMI records mailroom. He sought opportunities to do more and maintained his focus while, step by step, he climbed the ladder to fame.

Former head of Paramount Pictures, Barry Diller, also began his career in the mailroom at the William Morris Agency. He set himself apart and did more than what was expected in his position. It proved out in the end because, currently, he is chairman of Expedia, Inc. and IAC (InnerActiveCorporation), and is worth approximately two billion dollars.

There is Famous Amos, Wally Amos, the founder of Famous Amos Cookies, who started out in the William Morris Agency's mailroom and developed from there to become the first black talent agent. He made his fortune by sending his chocolate chip cookie yummies to the show-business greats he met through his agency. They were the ones who backed his successful cookie company. Again, focus discovers opportunity, which leads to dream fulfillment.

These examples make it clear that you have absolute control over one thing: your thoughts and where you focus them. If you fail to control your mind, be clear, you will not be able to control anything else. Consider your mind your spiritual estate. Take care of it, protect it, and use it with deliberation. You were given will power for this purpose.

The ability to control your mind is the result of self-discipline and habit. You have two choices: control your mind or it controls you. There is no halfway measure. The most practical method for controlling the mind is the habit of keeping it busy with a definite purpose, backed by a plan and action.

If you observe successful people, you will note that they have control over their minds and do not let others' negative input take up space. They direct their minds toward the attainment of definite objectives. Without maintaining this control, success is not possible.

Here are a couple examples of people who stayed focused, no matter what.

E.W. Woolworth was told that he would go broke running a store on five- and ten-cent sales. But Woolworth, centered on his goal, knew he could do anything within reason, and he kept his mind focused. This included keeping others' negative thoughts out. His success with the "dime store" is legendary. It was the precursor of the Dollar Stores, which now sprinkle the United States. Yes, Woolworth proved his point. Someone can be highly successful by concentrating on making lots of small sales.

Military leader, George Washington, was informed that he could not hope to win against the vastly superior forces of the British, but he believed otherwise. He masterminded his success through clever strategies. Consequently, he succeeded against a larger force by focusing on strategic action. He kept his goal of defeating Britain foremost in his mind in order to create a free nation.

There is a process called *multi-tasking*, which is revered in the world today. This means that people try to do five things at once and call it productivity. The problem is that these people don't remember doing any of it. Advocates of this process create a mind that is scattered, unfocused, unproductive, and definitely not in the present moment. The most inefficient way to conduct your life and manage your time is multi-tasking.

The belief that you can do two or three tasks at the same time and be effective is a hoax. You write a letter and talk on the phone while listening to the radio or watching television. What do you register of any of it? The mind glides from one thing to the next and back again, remembering little. You are living a less than memorable life. Great inventors, creators, designers, businesspeople, and leaders are focused. Greatness requires clear vision, knowing what you are doing and where you are going.

One of the methods I used to develop strong concentration (reflecting strong intention) was to gaze at a candle for ten minutes. I did this daily. The idea was that, if your attention left the candle, you were to make a mark on a piece of paper and return your focus to the candle. Sounds easy, right? Try it and see what you think.

My experience, after performing this exercise for approximately six months, was that the mind is a wily beast and will wander off at the slightest provocation. Yet, even with that fact intact, there was still vast improvement in my ability to stay attentive to a subject until I was finished. After doing this exercise for a year, I had developed strong concentration skills and was able to hold to a subject as long as needed.

Why is this important, you ask? It is important because we are creative beings. To utilize and maximize our creative output, we must be able to concentrate. People who play loud music and talk on the phone while immersed in a project are self-sabotaging. On the other hand, individuals who set their mind on a goal and are not deterred, accomplish incredible things.

We saw this phenomenon during the 2016 political campaign for President of the United States. Donald Trump focused on the prize. He continually affirmed, *We are going to win and we are going to win big*. He never lost that view and his creative mind, along with the creativity of others on his team, led him to work in the right places and seek the endorsement of those in greatest pain and hardship: the disenfranchised, those out of work, those in diminished fiscal condition. He won the election. Can we learn from this? Yes!

Learning to center on your objective without distraction (or doubt) provides an incredible command that ultimately yields the result you seek. Yet, there is another reason, perhaps more important, to develop strong concentration skills, and that is to cultivate "inner vision."

For example, those who have meditated for a long time (many

years) tend to possess the capacity for objectivity and lightness of spirit. Detaching from the material world to experience inner vastness is an amazing tool that not only helps you release anxiety and stress, but also supplies deep insight and peace. This is called mastery.

Quantum physics makes it clear that, inherent in each person, there is sufficient power to light an entire city. That is a lot of awesome power. Yet, how do we use that power? Many people use their innate power to stay small and limited. This book is for the ones who choose to harness the power they have been given in order to create an amazing life. This can be building kingdoms or learning how to live in our Heavenly Kingdom while we occupy the world. It is a choice. Both offer great learning possibilities.

In this book, you will discover principles and techniques to control your wandering mind and cultivate qualities of vision, intuition, and resourcefulness. You may have noticed, there are suggested activities at the end of each chapter. They will help you put these techniques into play to create the results you desire, along with a life directed toward truth, success, peace, and understanding.

Understanding the mind is a great adventure. Learning how to use it well will give you power. Not power over others, but power over self. When you are intensely focused, anything can be accomplished. That is mastery. The tools supplied herein will help you attain the control you need to create the life you desire.

To What Are You Feeding Energy?

All of us are living with dogmas that we accept as truths.
When one of these is overturned, there's an initial gasp,
soon followed by a rush of exhilaration.
Deepak Chopra

A few years ago, a movie came out starring Russell Crowe in the role of a brilliant mathematician, John Nash. This movie, called *A Beautiful Mind*, relays lessons about managing the mind, which can help every person.

The movie posed a biographical sketch of John Nash, who suffered from a mental condition by which he saw people who no one else could see. In the dialogue, Nash comments that *one must choose to what he gives attention*. In his schizophrenic state, Nash would see imaginary people who instructed him in various activities. His issue was that he allowed these figures to have relevancy and authority over his familial and university responsibilities. By doing that, he posed danger to himself and others.

Nash had to work hard to gain authority over his misdirected mind. As he progressed in his treatment and recovery, a colleague asked him if he still saw "the people that other people don't see?"

Nash responded, "Yes, but I don't feed them energy. It is kind of like fear. You can feed your fear energy by giving it attention, or you can just ignore it. It needs energy to live. If you ignore it, it ultimately goes away."

In order to heal from mental illness, Nash had to refuse to feed his delusions. Through dedicated effort, he recovered from paranoia and schizophrenia to become a talented, effective mathematician, parent, and teacher. His work in gaining control over his thoughts illustrate a personal lesson for everyone.

Many people seem dedicated to living in fear. They constantly focus on everything that is bad, imperfect or wrong, or even potentially wrong. In their downward gaze, they are unable to see beauty. Surrounded by the miracles of modern science, the ascetic wonder and inspiration of nature and the kindness and generosity of people, those people focus on and feed fear, hate, and neurosis. Yet, at any moment, by changing their point of view, a completely different picture of life could emerge.

It is amazing to consider, yet it is true, that one small act, accomplished with intention, can make the world a better place. You can go to work with the idea of making your place of business the best it can be. This intention leads you to answer the phone with a smile, see the customer as a blessing rather than an irritation, do extra things that make the surroundings pleasant: empty the waste basket, dust the furniture, bring in flowers or snacks. The point is that you choose what you "feed" energy." When you choose to feed optimism, enthusiasm, peace, calm, and positive intent, it turns out that YOU are the greatest beneficiary.

To what are you feeding energy? To what are you giving your attention?

Activity: Do this twice a day, once in the morning and once in the evening. Use your log or journal to review your day and note where and on what you have been giving your attention and energy. Make a list. Then decide if offering energy to these ideas, projects, or people is beneficial. Does it produce a worthwhile result? By paying attention and taking note, you will discover beliefs, activities, and people that need to be discarded. This process will make room in your mind and life for greater joy, productivity, and freedom. This is the work John Nash had to do, and it is the work we all have to do. Never waste your valuable resource of energy.

Attention = Energy.

Don't Poison Yourself with Negativity

Too many of us are not living our dreams
because we are living our fears.
Les Brown

Yes, it is true: Negativity is toxic. Negativity lowers your energy, immunity and vibration and creates resistance to love. Yet, keeping your thoughts positive and refusing negativity is a bit of a quandary, but it can be done. And, yes, it takes vigilance and discipline to accomplish.

The brain was established long ago with an original purpose of survival. It served as a guard dog, watching for danger and what lay beyond the next tree and rock cluster. Centuries later, we altered our sensory needs. We are no longer waiting for the next tiger to launch an attack and tear us limb from limb. We have advanced, so to speak, and revere sensory goals and desires. We chose direct action toward goal fulfillment instead of survival.

Hence, the need now is to re-condition the same brain and neurological impulse to seek pleasure and opportunity, instead of being on guard for an attack or to locate a safe, dry shelter before the storm hits.

As we identify with Spirit, the impetus is to expand our consciousness and move beyond fear, anxiety, stress, and worry as toxic thought systems. These toxic systems literally poison the mind and body. The drive should be to reposition to expansion. This would be a joyful exchange and opens every opportunity for growth.

Thoughts take many forms.

What if people don't like me" can be switched to *I like people and they like me.*

What if I can't succeed" can be transformed to *There is always a way to succeed and I will find it.*

I'm broke can switch to *There are millions of ways to make money and I'm in hot pursuit.*

Stress over any possible scenario can be altered in the same way. When you do this, you lift the body and mind to lightness, health, and the highest vibration. It is an everyday event to catch yourself in a negative thought pattern. Why is this? Because somewhere in your past, you experienced a moment where something wasn't going the way you thought it should.

For instance, your parents had an argument and you got scared that divorce was eminent, so you decided all arguments were bad and led to terrible consequences. From there, you froze when someone raised their voice.

Thus, from an instantaneous mental photograph, you formulated a lifelong pattern that has interfered with freedom, optimism, and openness. It could be that the last time you saw your kid brother, he was getting into a red car and later killed in an accident. Ever since, you can't get into a red car. None of this is rational. When you set up a negative belief system based on irrational conclusions, you are irrational, and your life becomes irrational. It all goes downhill. Yet, at the same time, it is all changeable.

Belief systems are not set in granite. You can re-remember an incident and change its meaning. You can forgive yourself for jumping to conclusions, and you can start over. You can let go of mental poison and clean the slate.

People argue and nothing bad happens. Some folks even enjoy arguing and think it makes their relationship interesting, even exciting.

We were trained in a fear-based society to protect ourselves from negative judgments and criticisms from other people, which puts our attention on other people instead of being who we are. The result is that when we find ourselves in potentially volent situations, we react to negative stimulus rather than responding to it.

To change unthinking impulses requires going back to our deepest desire. Do we want to live in defensiveness, blaming, and excuses or move to the peace and calm of our deepest mind (the Christ Mind, the mind of love)? To perfect our ability to overcome a tendency to jump to an imprudent stance, rather than thoughtful deliberate consideration, requires learning to take a moment to step back.

When we step back before taking an impulsive action, we are remembering that we have a choice. This confirms our spiritual nature. This considered movement is about choosing conscious intent. As this choice is made, we dissolve the ego need to defend, excuse, or place blame. It is a choice in freedom.

Many reactions are set up to evoke positive judgments from others. We point our finger at someone else. We disavow our responsibility, make excuses, and place blame elsewhere. In truth, there is no elsewhere and we only grow by recognizing our defensiveness as a sign there is more internal work to do. On the other hand, if I know that I am a good person with highest intentions for all, I relinquish any need to prove it to someone else. Reactions generally indicate there is no conscious thought present.

Thoughtfully responding is a conscious act flowing from a clear intention. There is no poison and no one is hurt.

Activity: Select an experience that you consider to be negative. Remember it and then look at it as though it was someone else's experience. Then look at it as if you were a young child at the time. Then look at the experience as though everyone else in the experience were young children. Keep examining the experience from every angle until you are able to see it as a learning opportunity instead of a deep wound.

Illusions: What They Are and How to Crack Them

A man's own self is his friend. A man's own self is his foe.
Bhagavad Gita

Look at dreaming. Our brain is designed for dreaming. Can you imagine how people create their ego illusions? Victimhood, for instance. The particular slant a person takes to support the idea of victimhood is to look at each situation from the point of *how I didn't get my fair share, how this situation went against my preconceived idea of how things should be, how I am being short-changed or ripped off, taken advantage of, etc.* In other words, it is all about ME!

Conversely, a *winning, successful person* will look to see *how he came out ahead, what gift the situation offered, how people are trying to be helpful, what strategy could be used to move ahead, etc.*

The idea that pain is bad is an illusion. Most people cannot grow without pain, as it is the catalyst that disrupts the ego. The ego wants security and attempts to find it by looking to the physical world, which is *never* secure. The material world is always changing. Change is the order of the day. The material world alters and adjusts, moment by moment, day to night, season to season, warm to cold, dry to wet, infant to teen to adult to old age. Endless change…nothing is stable.

Hopeless dreams and cravings (illusions) of the ego that control the person, create blocks to realization of connection to the Infinite Self and peace. Here are some beliefs (illusions) you may have taken on that permits the ego to run your life:

Accept what you get.

Don't ask for too much.

You should put others' needs first.

There is only so much money in the world.

Money is the root of all evil.

Rich people are arrogant, disdainful, selfish, blah, blah, blah.

You get the point.

Illusion is accepting the smallness of the ego. Ego illusion is agony and unhappiness because there is never enough. Its way is continual prodding with needs and insecurity. I need to be cuter, skinnier, drive a Mercedes, have more money, be popular, have a vacation, etc.

Serenity evades ego domination. All negative energy is ego. You desire peace and ego presents contradiction. You want a pain-free life and something doesn't go as planned. You break your arm and there is a contradiction. A judgment.

You want peace and simplicity and someone yells at you, kids are unruly, the check bounces, your friend drives you crazy. The illusion dwells on the fact that you are looking to the outer word as your source of peace, and it never will be. Peace is in your soul. You connect with it through the present moment, not from hopes that the material world will settle down and not from deciding how everything is supposed to be.

Emotional pain is always the result of ego decisions. You can change your decisions and, therefore, you can heal them all.

Understand that there are no absolutes. You don't have to be safe, or healthy, or happy or rich. Some of the happiest people live simple, unpretentious lives. The outer circumstances of your life are nothing more than symbols of your internal life. When you get quiet, you have access to an external/internal dialogue. Dwelling in stillness, you can see clearly, realize cause, and alter your course. You self-correct.

The blocks to peace begin to disintegrate when you discipline the mind by refusing to placate the ego. When you go off into unrelenting chatter, shock yourself by jumping into an ice-cold pond (shower). You are taking control and saying, *I, the spiritual being, is in charge here. I will choose what to concentrate on.* You take control of the chatter and refuse to listen. Place your attention elsewhere.

Power comes from serenity. You stop struggling against yourself. As emotional reactions calm, power comes up. This is how you heal and connect to transcendence. Ignoring negativity and random mental chatter releases fear. Give it attention and you empower it. When you ignore it, it withers away.

The ego is the same. The more attention you give its demands and worries, the more it controls you. When you ignore it, move to a higher focus (peace, for example), and use mental discipline, exercise, nutritional balance, meditation, as tools, ego is weakened. That is when it can be relegated to the back corner of your mind and ignored.

In this discipline, you discover your level of desire. Desire creates commitment. Commitment to regulate your lower (egoic) mind so that you can focus and connect to your higher mind is the way you will experience peace. Thus, examine your illusions to determine if it is time to let them go, if you want something more, if you want to create new goals and dreams.

Example: I put myself in situations to be criticized because my illusion is that people can't support me as a fringe dweller. My independence is an affront to them. They feel I am taking something from them (attention?). When I show my power, commitment, intensity, they are intimidated. As a result, I draw insecure people to me so that my drama/illusion can continue, so these insecure people will criticize because that is what insecure people do.

Here's a story that illustrates this illusion. Meryn *created* the illusion of *being cut off* in life because she allowed her passion to be cut off (believed she was not good enough). She listened to her parents and let their nitpicking critical attitudes have meaning for her. Thus, beyond decorating her house, she had no passion. Yet she knew she had talent and was good at loving and encouraging people.

So, the story goes, Meryn got lost when she placed attention on the outer material world (people and circumstances) and tried to make it have meaning and relevance. But she eventually re-connected to her True Self by accepting she had value as a person, that no one had the right to put her down and by having her own identity, separate from parents and husband. In the process, she dissolved the illusion of not being good enough. By reclaiming herself, she was able to live a life of passion.

How does Meryn's story relate to yours?

Vertical or Horizontal Thinking

We are not human beings having a spiritual experience;
we are spiritual beings having a human experience.
Pierre Teilhard de Chardin

There are two kinds of thinking: vertical and horizontal. The horizontal thinkers relate to cold, hard facts. They accept the world as it appears and believe only what can be perceived through the five senses. They limit themselves by unwillingness to examine broader possibilities.

On the other hand, the vertical thinkers cut through the outer appearance to go to the core of the problem or situation. These people don't accept limitation because they know that where there is a will, there is a way. Refusing to be a victim of circumstances, these people, instead, are their own masters.

Vertical thinking is *possibility* thinking. It pushes back boundaries. Vertical thinkers consider how to use or direct a situation to get what they want? It requires looking for options and alternatives. It uses the facts by going beyond them. Vertical thinking produces creativity, flexibility, and new solutions.

An example of vertical thinking is the factory in New England that had a terrible employee turnover problem. In a brainstorming session, set up to find a solution, a tired executive blurted, "Let's just cut off the legs of the employees so they can't leave." This blunt idea gave birth to the solution to their situation, which was to hire disabled people.

All successful people are vertical thinkers. They focus on solutions, not problems. They remain open and move forward in expanded new ways.

What problems have kept you trapped? Have you limited yourself by buying into appearances and the way it has always been done? Perhaps it is time to consider another way, to look for new possibilities and to try something new. The adage is: If there is a problem, there is also a solution for that problem.

Shape-Shifting to Become Your Amazing Self

The only way that we can live is if we grow.
The only way that we can grow is if we change.
The only way that we can change is if we learn.
The only way we can learn is if we are exposed.
And the only way that we can become exposed is
if we throw ourselves out into the open.
Do it. Throw yourself.
C JoyBell C

We live on multi-levels and exist as many layered beings. Example, I was raised by a nervous, neurotic mother. To be fair, she was also loving, kind, resourceful and dedicated. Living with a neurotic parent was a daily challenge, because she personified a philosophy I did not want. It was the glass-half-empty philosophy. Or, in her case, the glass was empty.

I realized early that I had no interest in living this fear-based belief system. At various times, I attempted to reason with her, debate with her, instruct her, and ultimately rebel against her. There also were times when I asked myself, *Why am I with her? How did I come to have such a frantic, miserable mother?*

It wasn't until years later, after I had forgiven her and myself, that I realized that *I am her*. No, I didn't fret and worry endlessly as she did, but I did possess the same critical, harpy, egoic voice as hers. Yikes! This is where we get into the multi-levels and layers of consciousness.

As I reflected back on my commitment to *not live her life,* I plunged forward with determination to create a different mental construct. I wanted a positive*, I-can-do-it-and-it-will-work* philosophy. I became unrelenting in my determination to find a way to live life according to that vision.

I sculpted the part of my personality that felt fear, and I developed practices that expanded the energy of love and peace. That led to a higher awareness that, in this life, I *needed* my mother to be the exact person she was because she embodied an important lesson for me: the ability to shape-shift. Of course, we all have this ability, but most people don't use it. The ones that do use it, succeed handsomely.

Shape-shifting involves taking the inherent characteristic or personality trait we have been handed (indoctrinated with) and molding it into a desirable attribute. The truth is all the things I disliked about my mother were *me.* I just demonstrated these characteristics differently. But I had the same base qualities, and I needed her presence in my life so that I could recognize this pattern. I needed her exact influence so that I could purge or reshape undesirable parts of myself.

No doubt, I had lived her life many times and this was the moment to make a change. I committed my current life experience as a turning point. I had finally gathered sufficient personal strength (perseverance, even stubbornness) to make the shift I desired.

What is this shift and how do we do it? My shift was *from* fear, worry, and anxiety *to* stability, stillness, peace, love and kindness. Perhaps it could be called a more centered life or even calmness. (People regularly comment that I am unusually calm.) Yes, I created that.

The point is, we live on multi-dimensions as multi-layered beings, and it was time to heal a tendency toward fear and helplessness that I brought with me from previous lives. This was the moment I was to heal false beliefs and illusions. My relationship with my mother clarified that I had no interest in following that path again, and it gave me the fuel to master change.

False beliefs*: I am powerless, helpless, unworthy. Other people are more important and capable than me. There is not a way to get through this. I am stuck. Other people have control and I don't. Blah, blah, blah.*

Perhaps you have been exposed to similar illusory mental concepts. It might be time to sculpt your characteristics and traits to radiate the amazing being that you are.

From a multi-level consciousness, we have lived many lives and had many experiences. That is not as important as what we've done with them. People live lives of abuse and chaos and grow from those experiences into exalted powerful folks who make great contributions in the world. Others in the same boat, remain downtrodden. What is the secret to shape-shifting from limiting beliefs or empowering ones?

Pay attention to what you feel when you are around negative people. Does what they say or do feel good to you? Bad? On target? Not quite right? That is where you start. If you follow something that feels wrong or dangerous, your body's instinctive alarm goes off, informing you you're entering dangerous territory.

So, when someone expressed fear, anxiety and negativity, I felt my inner alarm go off. This was not where I wanted to be. This was not my direction. It did not make sense. It was not how I chose to live in the world. This led to the practice of challenging those beliefs.

Belief: *I am helpless*. Challenge: Ho*w can I be helpless when there are resources available to help me?* Example: There are college grants and loans to use to get through school; tutors to help learn something; books and classes to suggest alternative methods; people who were willing to help; organizations that offer services, etc.

When you challenge a belief, you must look at it from various points of view to find truth. People too easily accept ideas that make no sense. How can you be worthless and everyone else have value? How does that work? What makes the difference? What qualities establishes worth?

You cannot accept others' beliefs randomly. Often children are indoctrinated (trained) to accept crazy, degrading, limiting ideas that are ruinous, and they go through life feeling guilty, dirty, ashamed, and unworthy because they do not realize they had a choice. There are many wounded, dysfunctional people, systems, institutions, and beliefs coming out of dysfunctional, fragmented, unhappy folks and institutions that must be challenged.

Indoctrination is how these false ideas are passed on. We are all responsible to shape-shift in order to become the persons we can be, rather than the ones we were trained to be. We all have the tools and resources available to us to do this.

Are You Stuck? Get Unstuck!

It is only after you've stepped outside your comfort Zone
that you begin to change, grow, and transform.
Roy T Bennett

Life is change. In fact, the only thing we know for sure is that everything is in constant movement: change. Each day is different from the one before or after, and it offers unlimited opportunities for evolution and growth. The antithesis of change is crystallization.

Being caught up in a crystallized thought pattern keeps you from growing, and it hastens age. The process of being stuck in a mind-set is called crystallization and occurs when a thought pattern becomes imprinted in mind and body. It is a kind of hardening that affects the way you move through live. When crystallized, you have no desire to see or understand from a higher perspective. Nor do you wish to improve.

There is a saying that the mind is great servant and a horrible master. It means that, when we let the mind dominate or give directions, we get in trouble. Whereas, when we let higher intelligence manage the mind, we can accomplish anything. Crystallized thought patterns mean the mind dominates. It happens when the mind is attached to beliefs or concepts about the way things are and being unwilling to consider other possibilities. It is certainly how bigotry and racism has continued through the ages.

In other words, the crystallized mind leaves no room for new perspectives. It is the mind that once believed the earth was flat, or arsenic is a healing agent, or there is one right way to do a thing. This mind is stuck and unwilling to consider another truth.

As life changes, your perspective and thought patterns change as well. Hopefully, you do not believe the same things today that you did as a toddler, a teen, or young adult. With time and experiences, you discover new ways of thinking and believing, which lead to new solutions. With openness, your thought patterns change and you expand in growth. This is why I have traveled to Europe and various countries around the world. I wanted to see for myself what was really happening and to get to know the people. It is why we seek new experiences instead of being a clone of other people's views.

When the mind is closed, we grow old. We lose the flexibility, adventure, and willingness of a child. Our refusal to test our limits, stay open, and expand and grow causes damage. A closed mind means no space for newness, and it means being stuck.

Children are flexible, open for adventure, willing to try something new. It is the rigid grownups who do not want to go to the beach for fear of getting sand in their shoes or who hesitate to hike or play ball because they might get worn out. Or, they don't want to travel because it is inconvenient. Stuckness means believing you must always have certain creature comforts or things must always go your way, or not have the inability to see possibilities if things do not go your way. Playing with new ideas is a huge challenge when crystallized in old ways. Plus, life is blocked from delivering new possibilities because you cannot receive them.

Can you think of areas in your life where you have become rigid and inflexible? Consider people, issues, politics, social rules, or situations about which you have formed an immutable opinion. These may constitute your personal issues by which you aren't open to gaining a wider perspective or deeper understanding.

Make a list of these and start with the first one. In time, go through the list one after the other. It could be illuminating, even fun. Sit quietly and go to your heart, sincerely surrendering to your heart's intuition. Your heart is your greatest source of new intelligence. It will open the door to new potentials and possibilities.

Here is the exercise: Select a situation where you are stuck in a mind-set and ask your heart for another perspective. Write down new perspectives. The point is to add heart intelligence and intuition to conceptual understandings so you can operate from a larger view and less limitation.

As you move through your day, catch yourself when you are in a rigid mind-set. In other words, when you have a set opinion and resist looking from another point of view. (You will feel resistance in your body when this happens). Then ask yourself: *Am I flexible enough to go to my heart with the issue and access a broader perspective?*

Crystallized thought is about protecting the status quo. It is fear-based. These rigid thoughts are so habitual, they may sneak by but, with dedication, you can catch them.

Below is an exercise to open your mind to expansion and new awareness. In time, you will move beyond thought crystallization to the fluidity of intuitive awareness. At that moment, your mind and body become flexible, and you have renewed your childlike sense of openness, willingness, and adventure, which stalls age.

Activity: Commit to trying something new every day. It could be as simple as checking out a new website or knocking on a neighbor's door to introduce yourself. Perhaps you can try a new recipe or shop at a different store. Keep a notebook of each new adventure and allow the experience to be an adventure. In other words, no judgments, just observations, and have fun.

Did you find something interesting on the new website? Did you find a common interest when you met your neighbor? Did you discover new choices when you ventured into a different store? Keep going. Keep notes. Take a class, try a new exercise, learn to dance! Enjoy newness in the same way that a baby does. A baby can explore an empty box for hours. Look with open eyes and wonder. See what shows up for you. Keep a notebook of observations.

True Freedom: Be No Thing

God is Love. I have learned so much from God that I can no longer call myself a Christian, a Hindu, a Muslim, a Buddhist, a Jew. The Truth has shared so much of itself with me that I can no longer call myself a man, a woman, an angel, or even a pure Soul. Love has befriended me so completely it has turned to ash and freed me of every concept and image my mind has ever known.

Hafiz

Every time we paste a label on ourselves or someone else, we are reduced. By identifying with a particular ethic group, political party, religious denomination, age group, gym membership, educational affiliation, or country, you minimize who you are. Each label or group reflects a particular energy.

If you are Islamic from Idaho, you evoke a certain image, belief, and behavior. Perhaps it is different than being a Hindu from Sydney, Australia. Every delineation places a limitation on the person to whom it is attached. Can you feel the difference between being educated at Harvard or the community college? Or between being a Peruvian Shaman and a

Methodist? Each determination draws forth certain symbols, beliefs, and categories. What if you decide to be *no thing*? That might include dropping the idea of being a human or a body and identifying, instead, as stillness or consciousness. You can see that stillness opens up vast territory.

As *no thing*, you don't have to fulfill requirements of occupying a certain location in the world, or being in a particular pattern of activity required to adhere to a certain ethic group, political party, or religion: crossing your chest before prayer, praying at a particular hour lying on a rug, working out at a gym five times a week, or sending money to support a specific cause.

There is nothing wrong with these activities when done with awareness and choice. When they are practiced by rote and as a way to fit into a community, rather than an activity of personal expansion, they are without meaning. They are activity and energy being directed without meaning.

Try this: close your eyes and breath with studied concentration. After ten or so observed inhalations and exhalations, begin to bring your awareness to who or what is breathing. No need to label, just observe. If you do this for a while, you will begin to feel more detached from the idea of identifying "I" with a label, and just notice that it is an awareness that is doing the breathing.

To take another step with this exercise, notice that between every inhalation and exhalation, there is a space, and between every exhalation and inhalation, there is a space. As you breathe, observe the space, and when you are ready, focus your attention into the space and be present there. As you do this, you will notice stillness. Be present in this silence and observe. While in the stillness, you will notice that gender, ethnicity, size, shape, and all other delineations have no meaning. You will begin to recognize that whatever you define as yourself is bigger than all the identifiers.

By cultivating the awareness of having no human identifiers, you realize that you are consciousness without a name or origin (family, country, party). You are having an experience of *no thingness* (no tangible thing).

Being nothing is vast, full and free. Practice it. When asked, don't define yourself as an ethnic group, political party, numerical age, race, religion or past experience.

Most people jump at the chance to give themselves these identifiers without realizing how they have shrunk themselves into tiny beings. In fact, your unwillingness to label yourself has nothing to do with anyone else because, along with being *no thing*, you are not judging anyone else's desire to fall into a specific category.

Mesmerism - Entrainment - Hypnotism

Whatever you focus on, controls you.
Jack Schwarz, Healer

You live in a media-rich world. Whether you tune in to *what's going* on via the latest webinar, news show, television, radio, or websites, you probably want information. The problem with being an information gatherer is that you may be collecting information that is toxic and even untrue.

Before World War II became an international event, Adolph Hitler spoke to a shattered nation, Germany. Germany had just lost World War I and was suffering from loss of confidence and self-esteem. This sense of loss made German citizens prime targets for a loud, authoritarian ruler, Hitler, who promised to bring greatness back to their nation. In the beginning, people didn't question his methods, which soon found their way into dictating every part of German life. If they had known the true character of Adolph Hitler, would the German people have acquiesced to his plan for "the purification of the human race?" No one knows for sure. We certainly hope there would have been second thoughts or even major doubts.

The point here is to recognize that Hitler's promises of a grand nation, relayed with charisma and confidence aimed at people who wanted redemption, set the perfect climate for the devastation of millions of people, just because they were the wrong ethnicity. This is a radical example of mesmerism, entrainment, and mass-hypnosis as the German citizens allowed their minds and wills to be taken over with the evil intentions of a madman. Yes, they allowed it.

Yet, this type of thing happens every day. If you have ever watched a pharmaceutical commercial, you will see the same process. A drug is presented to address a particular malady along with a video of happy people, laughing and playing together, indicating that they have taken the indicated drug and their lives are so much better for it. Or perhaps, you've seen a car commercial with a good-looking macho fellow driving his classy car. Very much in control! The message seems to be that, if you are driving this car, you are hot and people (women) will swoon with interest. It is a propaganda-type mental image. You get the point.

People have to protect themselves from falling for ideas and propositions that establish a need (within the mind) that does not truly exist. Of course, we see the same thing when everyone must wear a popular brand clothing or shoes. Nike comes to mind. Wearing the shoes means you are cool, you are with it. If you allow the idea to take hold, your self-esteem may be diminished by simply wearing the wrong shoes. How crazy is that?

Feeling good about yourself must *never* depend on what other people think or be so fragile that you take a drug or spend more money than you can afford on tennis shoes or anything else.

The word *entrain* means to board or put aboard a train. We can become entrained or board the train of other people's choosing if we are not careful. For instance, each person is raised in a certain cultural and/or ethnic environment and can become entrained to those specific habits, rituals, or belief systems. Often, they don't question these ideas. They simply *buy in* without even knowing it.

Perhaps Russians are taught to believe something, and Italians are taught something else. Americans something else again. Are any of them taught unity and to love their neighbors?

At the bottom of it all, you are responsible for what you put in your mind and the choices you make. Giving over control to a pharmaceutical company, a television commercial, or the current cultural ilk is dangerous. Look what happened to Germany and the entire world when one crazy man hypnotized an entire nation into believing that he could create a master race by destroying millions of people in incredibly grotesque ways. All they had to do was turn their backs and disavow what was happening in front of them, and most did just that.

To be fair, there is a positive side to mesmerism. It can be used to assist in teaching the alphabet, multiplication tables, the number of days in a month, etc. For instance, children learn the alphabet by learning a rhythm:

A B C D E F G,
H I J K L M N O P,
Q R S, T U V,
WX, Y and Z
Now I've said my ABCs.
Tell me what you think of me.

The same method is used to teach the number of days in a month:

30 *days has September, April, June, and November,*
All the others have 31,
Except the second month alone with 28,
until leap years gives it 29.

These rhymes are great teaching tools, and they can be used as such and are helpful in learning various concepts, like the multiplication tables, the alphabet, and other things we need in life. The point is, we have the responsibility to know when something is being used to support and expand life or to diminish it.

Ultimately, there are numerous ways that mesmerism or hypnosis is used in daily life. You can become a zealot in thinking one political party or method of worship or type of food is better than another and, thereby, be moved to violence on the subject. Certainly, we've seen destructive movements, like people harming folks that are different from them, enslaving people, groups like the Klu Klux Klan with their bigoted stance.

The question to ask yourself is: *Is this idea or way of being productive, expansive, or compassionate? Is it coming from a mind of love or fear?* This puts your own power of discrimination at the helm of decision-making.

You are responsible for what you do, how you think, and what you espouse to. Your life unerringly reflects the same result. You cannot lie to the Universe.

The point then, is to strive to be your best self and demonstrate your highest ideals of love, kindness, and expansion. As you do this, you lift your energy and encourage others to do the same. To live in a world of beauty, you must be that beauty. Or, as the great Indian leader Mahatma Gandhi said, *We must be the change that we want to see in the world.* We are responsible!

Here is a story that illustrates the idea of *entrainment*, introducing an idea into a culture that either increases or diminishes the culture.

The story took place in a coastal town, Monterey, California, which, for many years, was a pelican's paradise. During that time, as fishing boats came into harbor, the fishermen cleaned their catch and threw the offal to the pelicans waiting at the bay. As a result, the birds grew fat and lazy. Eventually, the fishermen found other uses for the offal, and the food supply for the pelicans dried up.

When this event occurred, the pelicans made no attempt to find their own food. They had become so dependent on being fed by others, they had forgotten how to fend for themselves. Soon, they were weak and thin. Some actually starved to death.

You might think that was the end for the pelicans, but not so, because an inventive person saw the problem and came up with a solution. New pelicans, accustomed to foraging for food, were imported from the south. These birds were placed among the starving pelicans. The newcomers immediately flew out into the ocean and started catching fish. Soon after, the hungry pelicans mimicked the hearty birds and ended their famine. The dominant pelicans entrained the starving birds and their natural instincts were restored.

On an everyday level, there are dominant people in our lives. Often, they are loud, boisterous, and attention-getting folks. Or, they have dominant positions in our lives as parents, grandparents, religious leaders, politicians, and so forth. Because they have a certain charisma, people follow them. Followers often want to be seen with leaders because it makes them feel important. These are the elements of a perfect storm for mesmerism or group hypnosis.

So, be careful. Check your own instincts and do not go against them. Is the message positive or negative, helpful or harmful? Does it enrich or diminish?

A dominant energy can entrain a less dominate energy. *You* can be the dominant energy in your life. You are the one to decide what you allow in your mind, what empowers you. That is self-mastery!

Recognize that this principle of empowerment has definite effects. If you choose to hang out with a crowd of naysayers, you can belong by becoming a naysayer. Unless you push yourself to become the dominant personality, you can relinquish your mental conditioning to negativity. People do this all the time and they make up lots of great excuses for yielding. *I've known this person (group) my whole life. They are like family to me. These are the folks that raised me, blah, blah, blah.*

The excusers do not see beyond the immediate comfort of long-term relationships, even though they are negative and diminishing. They have not put their personal expansion and their group above habit and comfort. Nor do they set boundaries with their cultural family. By letting others choose the path, they relinquish their authority and control. It is a big loss and predictable.

Ultimately, to achieve self-mastery, you must be attentive to mental habits and cultivated routines. If they distract from your purpose or goal, adjust them accordingly.

Who is the most dominant person in your family or at work? What control do you observe? Who have you let be dominant in forming your views of the world?

You can also use the principle of mesmerism to entrain to the mental image of someone you admire. Do you aspire to be strong, charismatic, and wise? Then study people who possess those qualities and let them teach you what it takes to be that person.

Activities:

Create a mantra or phrase for yourself. Repeat it often. It will serve as a mental reminder that you are *the dominant person in your life* and you are choosing who and what you want to be.

Example*: I am a success machine. I always find a way. I set a goal and I attain it. I am fueled by the Holy Spirit.* One person I knew said: *Money loves me!* (And it did.)

Designate one or two people you can use as inspirational symbols for the kind of person you wish to become. Study their characteristics and actions: optimism, honesty, authority, integrity, follow-through, positivity, etc. Reflect on how you might display these. Make these images your own. In other words, find *your* way to demonstrate the qualities you admire. Essentially, you are using these folks as a template for designing yourself but, remember, you are you and not them. Thus, you will express your desired qualities in the way that works for you, with authenticity.

Chapter 4: Your Personal Self – The Courage to Be YOU!

Managing Emotions for Peace of Mind

He who controls others may be powerful, but he who has mastered himself is mightier still.
Tao Te Ching

There is a story about a rider and horse that came galloping down the road. It seemed as though the rider had somewhere important to go.

Another fellow, standing on the roadside, shouted, "Where are you going?"

The man on the horse answered, "I don't know. Ask the horse."

The horse symbolizes our habitual energy. The story depicts how we usually live at the mercy of old habitual energies and patterns that have been established mindlessly by our surroundings and not by conscious intent. Thus, your horse, your habits pull you along, making you run here and there without even knowing why. If you stop and ask yourself, *Why am I running around so much?* you might have an answer, but it will never be a good one. You are just used to it. That is how we've all been taught to live.

If you ask people why they are a Lutheran, Baptist, Pentecostal, Presbyterian, Democrat, Republican, blue-color worker, business owner, horseback rider, poker player, or anything else, much of the time, the answer will be because their parents were those things, because they were raised that way, or because they had always done that. In other words, they don't have a good reason. They are simply following the habits of their upbringing. As much as they gallop here or there, proclaiming this or that, it gets them nowhere. Their claim to fame is being busy.

You need to take the reins and let the horse know who is in charge. You're the boss. You have always been the boss. So, start acting like it.

This story is also a metaphor for how we let our emotions run away with us. We have established patterns of reacting to things without clear, focused intention. To be the boss, we have to govern and direct, not suppress our emotions. We have to calculate when and how we react. To do this, we must discover the bigger picture of emotional management.

Our thoughts are electrically charged and our feelings are magnetically charged. Our brains evolved biologically from the past and are rigidly programmed with tribal beliefs and memories. Consequently, emotional reactions are also programmed from past orientation. We tend to repeat the same circumstances over and over because they are the ones imprinted in our psyche. It is redundancy to the fore.

If you want to expand your present and future experience, you must change the pictures in your mind. If, for instance, you would like to be rewarded more abundantly in your work but relate to an old image of *low wages* and *being passed over* for promotion, you would have to create an impassioned, *deeply felt new mental movie* of being applauded and appreciated at work, thus abundantly rewarded. You would have to feel jubilation when you receive your paycheck, and internally experience the pride of work and promotion. You would have to feel yourself smiling, joyously dancing in celebration.

This new magnetic-feeling energy would have to be repeated until you have replaced the old images of lack and discouragement. This is your mental movie. Don't wait for someone else to create it. They won't create *your* movie. But they can be a participant in it.

As you go through this mental movie, you are altering your neurology and, as your neurology adjusts, your body functions better. Overall, your health improves. The body was made to operate in high energy, in joy. Notice that babies are happy until taught otherwise. The happier you become, the better you feel and the more resourceful you become.

An interesting fact is that the mind and body do *not* know the difference between a real or an imagined experience. So, as you live in this new movie/broadcast of great reward and abundance, your mind, body, and neurological system accepts it as real. The more you enter and feel the movie, the closer you identify with these new circumstances, and you will, ultimately, see the manifested results in your life as opportunities show up to fulfill your desires.

Many people won't imagine a new life because they are afraid. They are so used to living a certain way, even though it is not a happy existence. They are intimidated with newness and will not venture into the unknown to create something new, even though they really want it. It does take courage to gamble on a new way or to travel a new path. Sometimes, the situation has to be so bad that a resistant person finally gives in and tries something new. That is the painful approach.

Emotional Genius

The sky knows the reason and the patterns behind the clouds,
and you will know too, when you lift yourself high enough
to see beyond the horizons.
Maya Angelou

Emotional genius or idiot? That is the subject of Karla McLaren's teachings on emotions. Respected author and healer, McLaren, instructs us that, *Emotions are celebrated and repressed, analyzed and medicated, adored and ignored, but rarely, are they honored. Yet, when understood, emotions reveal practical tools that we can use to stop struggling in relationships, family, career, and personal growth.*

For example, your anger holds crucial insights necessary to change a self-defeating behavior, like self-sabotage or stopping short of success.

Fear holds memories needed to effectively resolve a crisis. By plumbing deeply into your psyche, you will discover this gold and use it to create dynamic change.

Depression, by its very name, indicates repressing desires. It has also been said that body “fat” represents unfulfilled dreams. Yet, another sign of repression. By getting in touch with emotions, instead of running from them, you might embrace your most passionate inner desires, go on to fulfill them, and return, once again, to a natural state of joy.

What is it you really want to do or experience that you aren't letting happen? Observe your emotional reactions around people, events and activities, and you will note valuable cues regarding your *real* desires. When do you feel jealous and why? What activity brings you the most joy? Passion? Satisfaction?

Reverend Dr. Norman Vincent Peale tells a story of a young man who followed his successful father into the insurance business and, subsequently, failed three times. (A definite sign of being in the wrong business.) As the young man conversed with Peale, he gently, lovingly stroked the wood grain of a nearby table. Dr. Peale commented on the young man's interest in the table, to which he replied that he had always loved wood. As a tactile person, he found the textures, structure, and feel of it compelling. Furthermore, he loved creating beautiful wood pieces and furniture.

Dr. Peale suggested that he explore this passion to see what it might offer as a livelihood. The young man felt relieved as he left Dr. Peale's office. He followed through with the suggestion of using his passion as a livelihood and, eventually, became quite successful. He created a wonderful fulfilling career in the design, manufacture and sale of unique wood pieces and furniture.

Emotions offer a vast reservoir of information, linking you to your higher intelligence. By connecting with your emotional self, you can regain direction, key into your greatest talents, reenergize your body, and live an inspired life. Conversely, by thwarting yourself emotionally, you lose connection with your passion and fire.

According to McLaren, how well you use your emotional resources determines your emotional genius.

Mental Training: Move to the Heart

Nothing binds you except your thoughts;
nothing limits you except your fears;
and nothing controls you except your beliefs.
Marianne Williamson

The whole idea of not having control over emotional reactions is a misnomer. Of course, you have control. You are always choosing. Just because you have reacted to something in the past, it does not make you vulnerable to reacting to it in the present. You no longer have to succumb to anger, resentment, or depression when faced with challenging events. In order to take ownership of your emotional self, you must train the mind and have the forethought and dedication to alter old emotional pathways.

To believe that outer circumstances control your reactions is a way of giving up and living as a victim. To change this, you train yourself to become non-reactive. You teach yourself to look deeper at what is really happening and choose another way.

Start with intention. If, for instance, you choose to be peaceful, then that must become your dominant thought. You must commit to it. You must choose peace over and over, even when stressors appear to taunt you.

Emotions trace back to beliefs. Much of the time, you have been trained with illogical, irrational beliefs that cause you to feel out of control. You feel a bit crazed because you are attempting to manage outer circumstances and other people, rather than yourself. You can affect yourself and are required to do so, but you cannot rule the external world or other people.

Start by observing your reactions to an event, comment, or person, and trace it back to a mental construct that you have accepted as truth. For instance, if you believe that everyone should or must get along, and you then notice people fighting, you will have an emotional reaction: anger, upset, sadness. Why? Because fighting goes against your idea of peaceful cohabitation.

Another example involves the ideal that everyone should be polite or considerate. Then when you witness someone who does not follow that edict, you become irate, upset. Why? Because your belief has been violated. Again, you are focused on what you cannot control, which is other people, rather than on what you can control, yourself.

Of course, there are positive emotional reactions as well. You might notice an act of kindness or generosity and find it sweet and compelling. You may react in a joyful manner. However, just as with negative emotions, the same thing is true about positive emotions. You *believe* that kindness is good, so when you observe an act of kindness, you have a positive emotional reaction. Although it is fortunate to experience a joyful event, the underlying truth still holds true. The basic premise of mental training is to decide what you choose as your own state of emotional stability and stay true to it, not create automatic responses to other's actions or words.

Day to day, you have thousands of opportunities to observe and react to events and people. There will be many who don't agree with your values and beliefs. People who are unkind, critical, angry, and or resentful, represent but a few stressors that can evoke emotional reactions. In that way, you are ever-experiencing a world packed with a myriad possibilities and you get to choose how to operate with all these variants: career situations, relationships, family, technology, schedules, daily tasks, everything. Before you turn your nervous system to mush, get focused and develop techniques to manage your own emotions.

Thoughts have energy and so do emotions. When we have a thought, energy is instantaneously transferred to the emotional body and then the physical body. That is why we feel them in our bodies. Yes, when you feel happy, your body feels light and open. When you are angry, your body tenses up.

Therefore, by managing our thoughts, we also affect our emotions and our neurology, chemistry, and musculature. Ultimately, we are managing our health.

Stressful reactions are draining. They rob us of energy and joy. But, as decision-makers, we have the ability to adapt to challenges, including stressors, and remain peaceful. It comes down to supervising ourselves instead of the world.

Often people wait until they are alone, in a quiet place or on a retreat, to re-group and de-stress. Retreats are great, but we can't wait for the day, hour, or yearly event to let go of stress. Waiting is the same thing as shutting the barn door after the horse has escaped. We need methods to re-set ourselves *before* the damage is done.

Self-mastery involves being in the moment and managing your business as it occurs. After experiencing a tense moment, you may feel drained and need to re-collect the emotional, mental, and physical energy lost to your system. You can learn to do this quickly, with the least amount of damage. Otherwise, you can easily accumulate degenerative effects in the body, nervous system, and mind.

What I refer to is the ability to *step back in the moment*. It is a matter of training and discipline. As you observe then manage your emotional state, you conserve a lot of energy and preserve health. You can ultimately use this energy to be creative, have fun, and live a fulfilled life.

Can you remember a time when you changed your attitude toward a person or situation and everything turned out better than you expected?

A twenty-four-year-old man was gazing from a train's window. He shouted to his dad, "Look, the trees are going behind."

A couple, sitting nearby, felt pity for the young man's childish behavior.

The young man's dad just smiled.

"Wow. Look, Dad, the clouds are running with us."

At last, the couple could not resist and leaned forward to ask the father if he had taken his son to a good doctor.

The father smiled and said, "Oh, yes, I did that, and we are now returning from the hospital. My son has been blind from birth and he just got his eyes today."

In this story, you can easily assume one thing, then change your judgment on a dime after gaining more information. You might start with annoyance, shift to humility, then gratitude.

I chose this story to illustrate the fact that you can radically change your view of things, if you give yourself a moment to process your thoughts and feelings. Take a minute to record some events in your life where you quickly changed your perceptions and adopted a radically different attitude. Perhaps you thought a woman was aloof and unfriendly, then you found out she had just lost a loved one and was grieving. As you remember a few of these incidents, you will be reminded that judging too quickly is a mistake.

Next, think of a time or two when you were peaceful, relaxed, and happy. Mentally photograph one or two of these moments for future reference. You want to be able to recall these at a moment's notice. Remember the feelings that accompany these memories. For example, you may be sitting on a beach and watching the waves roll rhythmically to the shore. You feel peaceful and awestruck at the beauty and power of the ocean. Perhaps you are holding your child, sleeping peacefully in your arms. This fills you with comfort and gratitude.

Here is a step-by-step process to practice. Remember, practice makes perfect. When a demanding circumstance occurs, such as being stuck in traffic or the boss is in a bad mood, step back, place attention on your heart, the center of your being, and breath. Then quickly, recall the peaceful or happy memory or think of someone you love. Keep your attention there. Do not budge. All of this must be accomplished in seconds.

Your heart is your love center. Your heart energy is love, nurturing, kindness, and wisdom. When you move from head to heart, you immediately change your perception. Here are the steps:

Recognize the stressful feeling.

Shift your focus by stepping back and moving to the heart.

Breathe.

Remember a happy moment or someone or something you love. *Feel* it.

If speech is necessary, speak honestly from your heart.

Put this technique into practice at work, at business meetings, when late for a meeting, at a restaurant, in traffic, in line at the grocery store, at home with your family, and whenever you meet a challenging situation. Put this into practice all the time. Soon, peace will become your dominant energy and focal point, and you will have achieved mental-emotional stability.

Personal Deception - The Stories We Tell Ourselves

Watch your thoughts; they become words.
Watch your words; they become actions.
Watch your actions; they become habits.
Watch your habits; they become character.
Watch your character; it becomes your destiny.
Lao Tze

One of the things that adds tremendous stress to one's life is the stories one tells oneself, along with the impact the stories have on the quality of life. I knew a woman who was in her seventies and, within an hour of meeting anyone, she would tell the person that her mother had died when she was ten years old. Now, it was true that her mother did die when she was young, but what purpose did it serve to educate random people to that fact? What need was she fulfilling?

She used this story to rationalize various developmental issues she had not dealt with. She did not feel she had a role model for femininity. (What about television, movies, friends, relatives?). She believed she did not know how to be in an intimate relationship. She felt awkward about relationships in general. Thus, her story: Why am I not in a relationship? My mother died when I was ten. Why have I done this or not done that? My mother died when I was ten. And, so it goes.

Most people have stories they tell themselves. I have heard lots of them.

I need to keep the job I have that I hate because I can't make this much money anywhere else. (Result: misery and stress) *My parents taught me to be humble, never toot my own horn or say what I can bring to the table.* (Hence: no career advancement.) *I must stay in this abusive relationship because who else would want me.* (Result: low self-esteem and misery.)

These stories either increase or deflate energy. Your story expands or depletes your self-opinion and confidence. Stories can keep you hooked into anxiety, establishing a position. For example, *I always get nervous around people; I am awkward, shy, introverted, backward, not good enough, not that smart, etc. I am Italian, Jewish, Albanian, European, a daughter of the American Revolution*, you name it. People use these labels to identify themselves. The labels conversely create limitation. With limitation comes stress. Each label carries a meaning, or it wouldn't be used at all. We provide the story to define who we are, then we are trapped by it.

When the woman who lost her mother at ten tells her story, she is explaining why she hasn't grown beyond the challenges of her early life. She has convinced herself that she cannot move beyond the stilted image she has created of herself and, yet, she has accomplished a lot and become strong as she has learned to navigate life without the nurturing influence of a mother. She really doesn't need to keep telling this story. She actually has grown beyond it.

When you tell "my story," it is important to note if it has become a prison, a safe haven, an excuse, or a jumping off place. Just because you were born an orphan and spent years in foster homes and orphanages (like Wayne Dyer), does not mean you are any less equipped to manage life than someone who grew up in a Father-Knows-Best family. Living within various cultural, ethnic, locational stories can squeeze you to follow traditions and cultural patterns that are not right or a bad fit for who you want to be. If you confine yourself within the story, you may not have room (space) to explore new, creative possibilities.

Consider the stories of your life. How do you feel about them? Do they serve you? Is it time to let go or look at them from another point of view? Is it time to possibly resolve them? Rewrite an old story or create a new one? Are there challenges and difficulties you have blamed on external conditions or other people when what you are dealing with is just a story that needs revision? Have there been opportunities you lost because you were attached to a story that precluded taking advantage of them?

Observe your stories. You speak them all the time, to others and to yourself. It could be a poor-me narrative that has been there a long time and has repeatedly gotten in the way of living a joy-filled life. *Oh, wouldn't you just know that I would get a traffic ticket, house fire, released from a job, lose a friend, etc.* (Name the pain.) This victim narrative keeps you small, miserable and anxiously waiting for the next shoe to drop.

When you catch yourself in *story-mode*, step back and ask yourself if this yarn you've been telling yourself is making your life better or worse? Is it increasing or diminishing your stature and happiness? Is it blaming someone else for your circumstances? If the answer is yes, the story is generating angst, self-doubt, and stress, and it has to go. You are the one who can change it, revise it, eliminate it, and move on. As you master each story, you will find it easier to live without drama and judgment. You will be able to look for potential in each circumstance and be willing to address it as a matter of growth.

With each step, you become calm and peace grows.

Action: Rewrite your story.

Perspective - Your Choice

You can, at any time, decide to alter the course of your life—
no one can take that away.
Any person can choose to activate real directions of the self.
It is true for every individual that, at any moment,
he can choose to become himself.
Clark Moustakas

Remember the story of the bricklayers?

When asked, "What are you doing?"

One brick layer said, "I'm earning a living."

The next retorted, "I'm laying brick."

The third bricklayer stated, "I'm building a great cathedral."

The last bricklayer brought pride, joy and appreciation to his work. He went home satisfied. Which one are you?

Once, I met a tire salesman who, when approached for tires, responded with enthusiasm. "Yes, I can help you." He smiled broadly and relayed friendliness, eagerness, willingness to be of service. He judged his work to be important for he was helping people. His customers were served with tires and positive energy. He and they went home happy (and safe), he, because he gave 100%, and they, because they were made to feel special.

You have it within you to do the same. You can build a great monument or work for a paycheck. The rewards are drastically different. You are the only one who decides which it shall be.

An everyday example would be a homemaker who approaches meal preparation for her family with boredom and obligation. The meal might be nutritious, but the most important ingredient, love, has been left out. From appearances, her family fairs well enough, but how much better (and more fun) would it be if the food were served with enthusiasm and love? This doesn't mean every meal must be a feast, for there is much to be said for simplicity, especially after a long, active day. It also does not require extra effort to imbue whatever you do with love. This can be as easy as having a clear intention and performing with positive attention.

In our fear-based world, we have been taught to work for money. Yet, psychologists have proven that, for most people, money is not the prime motivator. The majority are inspired by recognition. Even the simplest acknowledgment given another can have a dynamic impact and literally turn a negative situation or relationship into a positive one.

Working for money as the only goal can be uninspiring, flat, uncreative, and joyless. Why? Because *you* are not a factor in the goal. In that case, you are not allowing work to bring you joy. If you sell insurance with the idea of making a financial quota, you are always looking for the next sale. Your interest in serving your customers is overshadowed by the need to meet your bottom line. In time, you don't care if your customers' needs are met or not because you are busy competing with last month's stats.

In other words, you've lost heart, soul, and passion for your work. You've become an insurance robot, spouting proposals and collecting revenues. Customers become numbers, not names. You measure success by how much is in the bank, rather than providing excellent service. *Did I touch lives? Did I help?*

Take an ordinary service, product, or activity and add something that makes it magnetic and irresistible. Add positive energy, like enthusiasm and appreciation, and you will find your job becoming fun. Your likelihood of getting a raise or promotion escalates along with your energy and future possibilities. As you continue expanding your knowledge, skills and service, you will be the biggest benefactor.

What activity, event, or work are you providing? Approach it with openness, appreciation, and as an opportunity to express your creativity and love. Then, step back and notice the results. First, did you enjoy it more? Did others? Which approach gives you the most satisfaction and fulfillment? Which approach helps you get up in the morning? Are you building a cathedral or just putting in your time?

Know Who You're Dealing With - The Critic or the Performer

Anything that makes you weak –
physically, intellectually and spiritually – reject it as poison.
Swami Vivekananda

This chapter assists in helping you understand your choices as the observer. First, recognize that the mind is your power source. Spirit channels energy into the mind, and you use this energy to think, motivate, and accomplish. To develop mastery, you must understand the mind and take command. In this way, you embrace the daily choices you face, which directly determine the quality of your experience.

A Course in Miracles describes three parts to the mind: the decision-maker, the critic, and the performer. This is where we deal with the critic and the performer. Other names for these parts of the mind include the ego and the True Self, or the contrived self and the real self. As you might recognize, one is negative and the other positive. One is fear-based and the other is love-based.

The critic offers judgments, opinions, and comments. It operates on a mental level. It plants doubt in the mind and disempowers. You might even call it the devil or deceiver. You know the critic well if your inner dialogue sounds like this: *You can't do that. Who do you think you are? You don't have the right education, contacts, skill, or perseverance. You will never amount to anything.*

Everyone has an inner critic and it never helps you achieve anything worthwhile. It is important that you recognize it and decide how to deal with it. And, you can consciously ignore it.

Beyond the critic, on a deeper spiritual level, is the performer. The performer takes action, knows you can do what you set out to do, doesn't analyze the problem forever, just keeps moving.

A good example of a performer would be the little boy who wants to learn how to ride his bike. He jumps on it with a determined mind, full ready for the attempt. If and when he falls off, he climbs back on undaunted. Perhaps he tries to ride it a different way. He keeps at his quest until he finally works it out. He doesn't count the number of times he falls because his focus is to ride the bike. Through all the trials and errors, he ultimately gains the experience, balance and muscle strength to do it.

The same would be true of hitting a baseball, setting up a computer program, painting a room, learning how to bake a cake. Each thing takes effort, determination, and consistency to accomplish.

Arnold Schwarzenegger is an example of a performer. He rose from humble beginnings, growing up near Graz, Austria. His family home was not equipped with electricity or running water, so he and his brother would walk for miles, carrying water to their home so they could bathe, clean, and cook. Arnold did not consider this a detriment or problem, but a situation to be dealt with. He did not see himself as underprivileged or a victim. He kept moving.

As a child, he saw a cowboy movie and decided that he was going to be a cowboy movie actor in the United States. He began moving toward that dream by becoming the youngest world-famous bodybuilder, Mr. Universe. He did this several times. From there, he followed the opportunities and, eventually, moved to the United States, trained celebrities, built a real-estate portfolio, and ultimately got his chance to act in movies. This was not a small accomplishment, considering he did not even know the language when he arrived in the U.S. On top of that, from movie stardom, he went on to become the governor of California. Arnold Schwarzenegger set his sights on his goal and began moving into action. He is the personification of the performer.

When it came time to write his autobiography, *Total Recall: My Unbelievably True-Life Story*, Arnold had a hard time remembering the timelines and particulars of his life. He had to call upon others who had kept photographs and notes. Remembering these past details was difficult because he had kept his focus forward. With each step along his path, he concentrated on where he was and where he was headed.

If you want to grow in awareness, it is important that you get to know both the critic and the performer. Many people get stuck in the critic and make their lives miserable. Nothing is right for them. Everything is cruelly judged. They maintain focus on the wrongs of the world. Yet, at any moment, they can become aware and make other choices.

Step back. Take note of your situation. Decide what action is needed. This is the decision-maker. If you are to achieve mastery, learn to distinguish fact from the dramatic conclusions of the critic. In any event, you are always the decision-maker.

It is important that you recognize your susceptibility to negativity. Often, it shows up in the other people in your life, perhaps even your family. Negativity is toxic. You must identify it and counteract it. Whether the negativity is yours or others, you have the ability to protect yourself and move beyond it.

There are many people who exist as lazy, indifferent, and willing to accept all suggestions that harmonize with their own weaknesses. It gives them an excuse to stay incompetent. Hence, attention is warranted.

Will power denotes the ability to use your will to make decisions. You must make decisions in life. What direction do you choose to go? By developing habits that cultivate positivity, you are being deliberate in building inner strength in the same way as Arnold Schwarzenegger and other performers. As you gain inner strength, you will not cave in to the critic.

As far as letting the critic dominate, the most common weakness is the habit of leaving your mind open to the negative influences. That includes the broadcast news. If you become unconscious of this tendency, you are cursed to work harder to achieve your goals. The idea is to spot negativity and close it off immediately so that you can live in high, positive vibrancy, not low, depressed energy.

This is the work that must be done to master your mind and operate as the conscious aware decision-maker. It is your life. Only you can make the best of it.

Ask yourself: *What do I know for sure in this situation? What do I know about this person? What am I making up, reacting to, or assuming?*

Don't decide what to do until you have sorted fact from fiction, truth from illusion. When you are caught up in the critic, you draw conclusions based on your past. *Who does this person remind me of? What is my issue? Am I experiencing jealousy or competition?* If you operate in the past, your deductions will not be accurate or forward-moving. The past is available as a memory to be corrected. The performer keeps his eyes ahead.

The performer has clarity about what he wants and the direction to take. When the performer spots an obstacle, the options are calculated. *What will it take to blast through this? Climb over this? Side-step it? Reduce it to rubble?*

When you decide your course of action, there will always be a way to accomplish it.

Activity: Here are some questions to help you discriminate between fact and fiction:

What triggers your inner critic?

When was it triggered last? Over what?

What is another way to think of this predicament and defuse the critic?

When does your performer come through?

What is the performer's dominant message?

What have you done about it?

What do you want to do about it?

Don't take Anything Personally!

If your happiness depends on what somebody else does...
you do have a problem.
Richard Bach, Author

In his best-selling book, *The Four Agreements*, author Don Miguel

Ruiz's suggests that you make a personal agreement with yourself to *never take anything personally.* That may seem daunting until you explore it fully. On close scrutiny, the idea of not taking anything personally offers tremendous freedom and joy. So, let's dig into the concept.

Maybe you had a critical parent, teacher, co-worker, or friend who, no matter what you did, found fault with it. If you got Bs on your report card, you might have heard, "Why didn't you get A's?" It didn't matter if this was a difficult class for you and getting a B was a profound achievement. If you cleaned your room, maybe your parent was able to find the one thing out of place. If you dusted the furniture, that parent might find the one spot still holding dust. When you completed a project, an authority figure may have pointed out an imperfection. Finding imperfections is not hard. There is no perfection in the external universe. It takes no extraordinary talent to do this.

The thing to realize is that people who are always looking for something wrong are unhappy with themselves. Their self-talk is always critical and, no matter what, there is never enough. Thus, the edict: recognize who you are dealing with and you will save yourself lots of angst. By knowing that you are dealing with a chronically unhappy person, you can expect criticism and, in time, it means nothing to you. Others are living their roles of the perfectionist, unhappy person and that has nothing to do with you.

If any of the outlined scenarios ring true for you, you may have developed a tendency to react defensively to criticism. Often, experiences of this type lead to the creation of an internal dialogue (self-talk) that mimics your parent. It can be harsh and critical. *I screwed up; I am a mess; I'm not good enough.* Or the inner dialogue may have gone into a *poor-me* defeatist attitude. *Why do I even try? I can never please him. I'll never get it right.* Or you may even think, *I'll never amount to anything.* Now, that is really going zonkers!

If criticism is your trigger and these statements replicate your reaction, you are being unduly hard on yourself. You have accepted another's harshness or bad mood and personalized it to reflect on you. The result is that you feel bad. This reaction becomes a neural pathway and a major block in achieving success and self-mastery. The negative undercurrent inhibits joyous relationships and pride of accomplishment and success.

The bottom line is this, the anger and criticism from your parents, spouse, siblings, and boss is *never* about you. It is a reflection, expression, and projection of them. Another way to say this is that a happy person is never critical or harsh, even when there are corrections to be made. A contented person doesn't put anyone down. Instead, that person makes factual statements. Mistakes are seen as opportunities to learn and to do better the next time. In other words, there is no reason to spew toxic anger or criticism.

Have you ever been in a crabby mood? No matter what happens, you don't like what is going on. The food isn't good and the service is worse. You don't like the way people drive. Your clothes look terrible. Your hair won't do what you want, and so forth. This state of mind is a result of being overly tired or discouraged. If you were in a better frame of mind, the food would taste fine. You probably wouldn't care what other drivers were doing. And you would be okay with your hair, too.

The point is that, when you are upset, you take this energy with you wherever you go. You radiate it. You reflect it. You impose it on everyone you meet. You're the one that sets people off wherever you go: the store clerk, the gas station attendant, other drivers, your spouse, and so on. Yet, your mood is about *your* discouragement, *your* discontentment, or *your* fatigue. It is not about anyone else. Others just happen to be in your line of fire.

Ultimately, *all feelings and criticisms are about the person expressing or projecting them.* That does not mean you are off the hook for legitimate corrections that need to be made. If you are late to work every day, that is a fact. Deal with it as something to correct, not a personal flaw with which you use to beat yourself up.

"What is the remedy?" you say. How do you take control of your reactions, rather than become immersed in other's negativity? The solution is to become aware of your own inner monologue, like, *I'm not good enough.* Then, pose a question. *Where did that idea come from and why am I accepting it?*

Challenge it. *Why am I not good enough? What proof do I have that I'm not good enough? What is good enough anyway?*

Years ago, I belonged to an organization where we put people on trial. "You are charged with being *unworthy* or *not good enough.* You are on the prosecution team. You *must* present proof to the jury that you are indeed unworthy or not good enough. Then the jury will decide if you have presented credible proof of the charge."

This was sort of like being a criminal in reverse. The plaintiffs had to prove that the charge was true. They had to present witnesses and findings to indicate that they were, indeed, not good enough. Of course, the whole experience was laughable because no one could do that. And when proof was offered, it was so lame, everyone, including the plaintiff, had to laugh. I loved the whole idea of putting people on trial to prove their self-proclaimed inadequacy. The trial put everything in proper perspective. It was affirmation in reverse, because the result was always that everyone was good enough.

So, *you* are charged with finding the truth. Find the real case behind the allegation that you are not good enough. Most of the time, you will discover that the proof you pose to substantiate your claim is shabby, indeed, or that you are thinking old habitual thoughts that are not and maybe never were relevant. You will then be able to step back when someone approaches you in a foul mood and recognize that the person is having a bad day. The person is in pain and expressing a mood that has nothing to do with you. What comes out of another's mouth is that person's pain or unhappiness, and it has nothing to do with you. The bottom line is, you cannot control others' emotions, but you can control your reaction to them.

If things go afoul with your plans, don't take it personally. If your event didn't turn out the way you wanted it to, don't take it personally. If it rains on your parade, don't take it personally. If someone thinks you are something you are not, do not take that personally, either.

Taking things personally is the ego's way of distracting you from experiencing your inner state of love. It keeps your mind in chaos, unrest, and anxiety, and therefore achieves its ego purpose of dominating your thoughts and keeping you from your Inner Light.

At the base of all human reaction is the desire for love and acceptance. Knowing this makes it easier to comprehend that when folks are *acting out,* it reflects a state of evolutionary infancy. You can react to spiritually infantile behavior or respond to it. Responding requires forgiveness. Would you be angry with a child for being upset if his toy breaks? Critical people are children in their development. In the space of a day, you may be called to forgive one hundred times. So do it.

Each time you forgive, you take another step closer to love, because each time you identify the ego's ploy to pull you from the Light of love, you deny ego control. As an individualized Being of Spirit, you are coming home.

As you understand and realize that you are a God-Being, everything else is overridden. All the ego voices mean nothing. If someone chooses to judge you harshly, it is on that person. To get involved in someone else's error spreads the energy of disillusionment and gives the negative judgment power. No need. Don't do it.

You can step beyond the small perceptions of others. You are a God-Being. Be still and know this truth. Then, you will see the child within the perpetrator and bless him, for he knows not what he does, while you are able to live in the Light of truth. You have raised your consciousness, and this situation has provided the means. Be grateful.

To live is necessary; to be offended is not. Only the ego is offended. Your True Self is unmoved by egoic affronts.

You can make a choice to cultivate feelings of peace and joy. Yes, it takes discipline and, yes, it is worth it. The dividends are enormous. As you train in not taking anything personally, you will begin accruing experiences where nothing will daunt you. That means you are free and at peace.

Activity: This is where you use your journal or log. Keep track of moments where you are triggered by someone's remarks or actions. Then ask yourself: *What about that event triggered my reaction?* Try to drill down into the feeling while asking: *What about me relates or agrees with what was said?* Keep pushing and soon you will reach an end point where a sense of release, relief, or knowing clicks in. This is when you will recognize your original erroneous belief and this is when you can, with ardor, decide differently. This is your point of change.

The Fragility of the Ego

Awakening is not changing who you are
but discarding who you are not.
Deepak Chopra

Many people get hung up on memories. These memories are their stories, and they keep themselves trapped in a mental loop that repeats over and over again. The emotional element in the stories translate into their present-day experience: the day their father abandoned them, when their best friend walked away to join another group, the time they were assaulted, beaten, or raped, when their teacher told them they would never amount to anything. They photographed this event, memorialized it, interpreted it, and stored it in their mental vault. It became the lynchpin for their own self-assessment.

These memories (stories) were experiences reflective of something within their psyche that needed to be healed. When reviewed properly, they can be a vehicle for growth. Without proper processing, these stories become mental traps that keep the person emotionally and spiritually thwarted. In other words, the individual has created an emotional wall behind which that person is stunted. All future experiences are interpreted through the same lens as the original painful memory. New experiences are skewed, misinterpreted, and internalized.

Claudia's dad told her that, if she achieved a certain ranking in her horseback riding lessons, he would treat her by taking her on a trip. Claudia loved her dad and worked hard to accomplish the riding status he required. Because she wanted to spend more time with him, she was proud to tell him that she had pasted her tests and achieved the agreed-upon status. Instead of being proud of his daughter, Claudia's dad told her that he did not make the promise and there would be no trip. Claudia was devastated and her self-esteem was crushed.

This is the memory that unconsciously arose in Claudia's mind whenever she was promised something by a man and he did not follow through. This mental story kept her trapped because she took her dad's broken promise personally. To her, it meant he didn't love her, she wasn't worthy, and he was a liar. By extension, men were liars. Because Claudia had never processed this occurrence, she did not come to terms with the fact that her dad's broken promises reflected *his* lack of character and had nothing to do with her value, worthiness, or goodness.

When she came to see me, she could finally step back and see what was really going on in her relationship with her alcoholic father. At that point, she could finally forgive him and herself for placing so much emphasis and self-esteem on his behaviors. As a result, Claudia found healing to a long-standing internal wound and was able to let go of the blame, shame, and guilt she had created from her original interpretation of this past event.

The truth is that, whatever her father did or did not do, had nothing to do with Claudia's value. When she understood this, she could walk from that memory/story clean, able to be her true self, an inspired, creative being of passion and determination.

Understanding that what people do or say is about them and not about you *is* key to loving yourself. The edict is that wounded people wound others. Claudia's alcoholic dad was wounded, and he lived from his wound and projected it to others. We all do this until we realize the deeper truth that we are in charge of our own well-being. No one can hurt us unless we let them.

Activity: To put this principle into play, *observe* your moods, behaviors, and thoughts. First observe, then make changes. If you observe anxiety or defensiveness, stop and get quiet. Sit with the energy. Sit in the anxiety, defensiveness, or anger. Breathe with it. Try to create acceptance as you do this. Don't judge it. Just accept the energy as it is.

Being still and without judgment creates inner space. This will allow you to see more clearly. Give yourself five minutes to do this. Perhaps you are making a simple event into a mammoth experience. Take time to evaluate it.

Next, adjust your mood. Identify with the peace that is in your heart. Yes, that's right. Go to your heart. There you can make the connection to Spirit and joy. Breathe with it. Be with it. Give yourself time. When you do this, stress melts away.

Do this a hundred times a day, if necessary. Keep bringing yourself back to *YOU*, your True Self, Love. In time, you will replace the old habit of reacting into a movement toward peace. Each time you do this, you are building a strong neurological structure, like a muscle. Standing in your truth will get easier and easier.

You don't have to take anything personally. As you learn this new way, it will become easy to forgive the crabby salesclerk, your disgruntled boss, your worried spouse, and even yourself. That is what Jesus meant when he said, *Forgive them, for they know not what they do.* That includes you, too. Sometimes you have to stop and take time to access what you are doing. By taking a moment, you can cease reacting. Soon, you will realize that it is not worth your time or temperament to ever take anything personally.

The Illusion of Control

If life were predictable it would cease to be life and be without flavor.
Eleanor Roosevelt

Control, control, control! Just when you think you've got things the way you want them, Whammo! Something beyond your control bumps into your life and throws you off-center. You can fantasize about how lovely life would be if things would stay put, but the truth is, nothing stays put or remains the same. The nature of life is change. The challenge, then, is to make peace with change.

Life is a path we travel: growing up, making and losing friends, education, meeting and losing people, challenge, disaster, success. But why?

Every experience you go through changes you in some way. Every person comes into your life for a reason, a season, or forever, and each help you transform. Every dilemma, challenge or opportunity you come up against alters you in some way. You decide how. That is how character is developed. You have the inherent right and opportunity to transform yourself to a higher state through these events, or you can allow them to victimize you. The results of these choices are evidenced in your life by who you are right now.

In other words, the quality of your life is the result of the character and philosophy you have developed on your journey. Develop kindness, empathy, perspective and tenacity and your life demonstrates the result. Choose bitterness, self-pity, victimhood and negativity, and your life reveals this as well.

Growing up in a large family in dire poverty, Dolly Parton could have easily given up. When the kids in her high school laughed at her confession of her hopes of becoming a country-western star, she became more determined than ever. Today, she thanks them for helping her stay strong and motivated. Parton was not going to let poverty or other people's vision of her get in her way. You don't have to let obstacles define you, either.

How is your journey unfolding? What qualities are you demonstrating? Are you who you want to be? Your actions reveal you!

You Can Do It! Failure Is an Illusion

Before you meet with success, failure is natural and necessary. As a baby learns to walk, it keeps falling down. Is this failure?
Master Sheng-Yen, *Being Natural*

There are lots of things you cannot control: the economy, the way others think or behave, the price of eggs, the Arab-Israeli conflict, Kim Jong-Un. It would be easy to become so immersed in the number of items you cannot control that you forget what you can manage: that would be *You*.

In a fear-based culture, there is a societal tendency to dwell on negativity. *What if this happens or that happens*? People ruminate on negative possibilities. You might notice it if you watch the news (or even the day-time soap operas where everything is a tragedy). People really think it matters, like *what John said to Kimberly or why Angela is sad.*

Unpleasant events dominate and it becomes vogue to talk about problems. It is easy to transfer this *victim mentality* to yourself. *Poor me. Life is hard! Blah, blah, blah.*

Eventually, with the preponderance of negativity, you get pulled down and feel lethargic, unmotivated, even depressed. Negativity results in loss of focus, movement, direction and energy *But*, it doesn't have to be that way.

We have all experienced moments of loss or failure. It is the measure of a person as to how that person chooses to respond to these. We can let each event that turned out differently than we had planned or expected become a terrible tragedy. We can believe that, with failure, we are losers. Or, we can deal with each experience (job, relationship, strategy, interaction) as an opportunity to pick ourselves up, learn something new, and adjust with a different approach. As Helen Keller once said, *Life is either a daring adventure or nothing at all.* In other words, no one comes out of the shoot knowing everything. The truth is that life is an ongoing experiment.

Take note of the people who failed in their missions before they saw any glimmer of success. Bill Gates is a prime example. Even though he is one of the richest people on earth, Gates had his share of failures. An example is his first business called, *Traf-O-Data*, which crashed and burned. Undaunted, Gates and his partner Paul Allen moved on to form one of the most profitable companies in the history of the world: Microsoft.

Former President Harry S. Truman also failed in business. He and his partner Eddie Jacobson set up a hat shop in Kansas City. America was in economic decline at the time, and the business failed, leaving Truman owing $20,000 to creditors. Instead of declaring bankruptcy, he paid back all the money he owed. It took more than fifteen years, and it set his character as a guy who fulfilled his responsibilities. Remember his famous remark: "The buck stops here."

Harry Truman was also defeated in his second term as judge in Jackson County, Missouri. Undaunted, he ran again and was elected Presiding Judge. Truman developed the reputation as a man of integrity. No doubt, the way he responded to defeat fed into that reputation.

We are all driving cars right now because of the genius of Henry Ford. His global vision was that consumerism was the key to peace. He acted on that idea by creating methods of mass production for inexpensive goods, high wages for workers, and systematically lowering costs. All of which resulted in technical and business innovations, including a franchise system for Ford dealerships. Yet, along the way, he had his failures. His Detroit Automobile Company went out of business and the Edsel car was not a market success.

Each of these people did not let loss or failure get in the way. They saw each experience as a stepping-stone to the next one and got stronger, more creative and savvier as they went along.

Albert Einstein failed in his college entrance exams. Thomas Edison had numerous (thousands) of unsuccessful experiments before finally perfecting the light bulb and other inventions. In fact, Edison used his failures to construct his successes. In his mind, each "failure" illustrated what did not work so he could discover what did. It was a process of elimination.

Abraham Lincoln failed in business twice, was repeatedly defeated for public office and had a nervous breakdown. These were a few of his many challenges.

All of these people failed according to the external facts. Yet, if you were to focus only on the things that didn't work for them, you would never guess their impact on the world, which was far-reaching and profound. They literally changed the way we live our lives.

Gates, Einstein, Edison, Lincoln, Ford and all successful people, refuse to pay attention to their failures, other than learn from them. They marched to the tune of their own drummers and lived their lives accordingly. They refused to let failure define or stop them.

The thing that holds people back is what they think they *aren't. I'm not smart, inventive, social, graceful, clever, witty, etc.* Turn this around and you can decide what you *are* and you, thereby, convert negative, static energy into forward thrust (movement and power). It can sound like this: *I am determined, persevering, forward-thinking, good at math, science, conversation, polo, etc.* To bring your energy up, you must agree to a positive self-image. This is how you tap into your source of inspiration and motivation.

Motivation comes from within, not from external people or sources. It is a force that moves you to action. Your belief about yourself is the starting point. If you believe you can achieve something, despite drawbacks and obstacles, you can. If you are sure that you cannot make it work, you are also right. Your decisions and self-view profoundly influence the outcome of your life. You can base your decisions on past failures, or on what you want to happen next and focus on the steps required to bring that result into being. Either way, you are in control.

What you control is yourself: your vision, determination, and desire. Take command and alter your destiny. Then, no matter how many times you fall down, you will keep getting up and eventually hit your mark. The edict, per Henry Ford is, "If you think you can, you can, and if you think you can't, you can't. Either way, you are right."

Benjamin Disraeli stated it this way: "The secret of success is constancy of purpose."

Audre Lorde stated, "When I dare to be powerful, to use my strength in the service of my vision, then it becomes less and less important whether I am afraid."

Psychologist Dr. Wayne Dyer said, "Failure is an illusion. No one ever fails at anything. Everything you do produces a result." His idea is that, if someone throws you a ball and you drop it, you did not fail. Instead, you say, "Throw it again." Soon you are catching the ball.

You make failure illusions real by identifying with them. If you decide, *I will never be able to catch the ball. I am a failure at catching the ball,* then you are a failure. Fear makes the illusion real. Fear can be eliminated by love. You can love the opportunity to learn how to catch the ball, how to write a letter, how to bake a cake, fix a car, or run a business. You can love the opportunity to be whatever it is that you want to be. Just keep practicing at catching the ball.

Fear knocked at the door. Love answered and no one was there. Ancient wisdom

The Challenge of Seeing Clearly

When people tell you who they are, believe them!
Maya Angelou

What constitutes seeing clearly? Author John Roger makes a simple yet profound statement: "Vision is seeing things as they are." How often do we see things as they are? It is a cultural tendency to falsify images, to look beyond current reality or, the opposite, to become so fixated on immediate gratification that we don't connect what we are seeing to the rational consequential outcome. In other words, actions or causes have future effects. These are "unseeing" tendencies that ultimately create disillusionment, confusion, disappointment and discouragement.

We have been rightly told to look for the best in people. This persistent search for the positive helps us feel good about ourselves and life in general. But we experience problems when our quest for goodness discounts negative qualities that are staring us in the face.

People have positive characteristics and they also have wounds. We honor the positive qualities and note the wounds. (Often wounded people wound others.) It is good to recognize the broad spectrum of each person and situation. In that way, we develop honesty and clarity to make the best decisions possible. As the Dalai Lama says, look at the situation from every point of view. Then you know what you are dealing with.

This is not to say that concentrating on weaknesses and flaws will help us produce honest assessment of an issue or person. That would be judgment. Yet, if you see one side and not the other, you are ill-prepared to act judiciously. It is not about judging. No need to judge. Just work on clearly seeing what is there.

At times, our desire for beauty is so strong that we mislead ourselves rather than face a blemished world. Somehow it seems easier, at least until we can deny reality no longer. We want a perfect world and sensitive, kind people. We want our children to be happy, successful, popular and smart. We want a well-meaning boss and a great idealistic company for which to work. We want that, but that doesn't mean that is how it is. There are many factors in play besides desire. If something doesn't work out as we wish, there is no necessity to react in pain.

Disillusionment is based on false images, which are grounded in erroneous beliefs that you've accepted and downloaded.

Belief: *It is important that everyone like me.* Not really.

Belief: *It is of dire importance that everything goes my way.* You'll manage if it does or if it doesn't.

Belief: *There really are things that I can't stand.* You've stood them to this point and you can continue to deal with them, if need be. If you had seen things as they are without judgement, not good, not bad, you could have averted the emotional letdown.

Delusion takes place daily with bosses, parents, children, friends, enemies, salesmen, waitresses, everybody. Our world is filled with false images. But you can re-establish reality by being honest. Go back to seeing things as they are. If you eliminate judgments, it is easier to perceive truth. Judgment narrows vision. As long as you put people or situations in a judgmental box, you will not be able to see all sides and it will deter good decisions.

All things exist as neutrals. The way you perceive and use the people and things in your life makes them good or bad. Of themselves, they are neither. You cannot say a car is bad because it has the power to kill. It is not the car's fault if it is used lethally. The car is neutral. The driver determines its constructive or destructive use. The same is true with electricity and guns.

You owe yourself honest, clear perceptions. That way, your choices become clear and you can continue to steer yourself in the direction you want: understanding each person, thing and situation to its utmost potential and giving the same in return.

Activity: When something doesn't feel right, it probably isn't right. When that happens, stop and write out a description of the situation and ask yourself what about it does not feel right? Check the motivation of each person involved. What are you noticing? Probe into the purpose of the situation and how it had formed.

By this time, you should have isolated a problem or discrepancy. Something about it does not fit with your morals and standards of behavior. Determine what seems off and make the proper adjustments. Leave a situation that is out of integrity with who you are. Stay and correct situations that are slightly out of balance. Say "No" when necessary and move on when necessary. You will be thankful when you come to terms with a person or situation that does not fit your criteria and standard of behavior. This is all about you managing your life!

Awakening to Who You Are

Life is really simple, but men insist on making it complicated.
Confucius

In short, authenticity is being who you really are. And what is that? You are the energy of the Universe. The truth of your being is in your heart. The mind wants to tell you otherwise, but the mind is only a vehicle that the consciousness of who you are, is using to experience in the outer world. It is a servant, a tool.

The material world is a vehicle filled with symbols and nothing more. It is a schoolroom where you can act out your karmic drama until you exhaust the ego personality and needs and sink gracefully into the love that you are.

Do you need to fall flat on your face? Do you need to see your worldly aspirations blow up to finally realize that what you seek is in your heart and not outside of you? If so, that will be the plan. Your level of resistance is the indication and determination of what must be, because the whole earthly journey is about waking up.

If you are in a job that you find draining and uninspiring, you must recognize that you are destroying your creative self each day that you continue. If you are hanging out with people who are toxic, you must wake up to the internal destruction playing out inside of you.

Being authentic means to connect with your greater self and express the energy it presents. If you are a chef, prepare food. If you are a comedian, stand before people and tell jokes. If you are a mathematician, be that. Naturally act out the energy that has been given you and do it in the most expanded possible way.

Just as the Buddha said, *I am awake*, you, too, are on a journey of awakening. You have been asleep and mesmerized by the drama and dance of earth life. When you find it taxing enough, you will turn within, and it is there that you will discover the love and inspiration you seek.

Will you miss the drama? No, because by the time you turn to face the reality of love, you will be ready.

There is no rush. You will arrive at the right moment. The suffering you have endured as you traveled the road to awakening will have prepared you. In some way, with all the nonsense of the ego, it will have worn you out. You will realize that, no matter what, you have never been abandoned. You have always been loved. Can you see with new eyes that life has been stacked in your favor? Every event and person have been a guide, each one with its message and lesson. All of it has been guiding you home.

Activity: Make a list of the people in your life, the ones you consider family and friends. Assign an attribute to each person. Make this real. Don't fudge. If the person is crabby or negative, make that the person's attribute. It can also be positive. Just be honest. When you have completed the list, ask yourself how you are demonstrating all of these qualities. Most likely, you are demonstrating them differently than the person in question. You can use this list to awaken to who you are being now. Do you want to make changes? Remember, life is a journey with lots of steps along the way.

Do Your Own Work

It is confidence in our bodies, minds, and spirits
that allows us to keep looking for new adventures.
Oprah Winfrey

You are the directing intelligence of your mind. As such, you decide your path. That means, even if you let someone else captain your ship, you have still made the decision for that to happen. Start by asking yourself, *What do I want?* If you are a person who hasn't asked this question before, you might find it daunting. But let it be simple. You want peace, quiet, orderliness, to accomplish some tasks, to feel good about yourself. Choose!

Choosing involves asking *yourself* what you want. It does not involve copying what other people want. This is a soul exercise. It is listening to your soul's desires and expressing them. These may be completely different from what is considered *normal.* In fact, there is no *normal.* It would not be doing what you *should* do via someone else's interpretation.

A big part of doing your own work is allowing yourself to be the unique being that you are. You first connect with what you *really* want, then you move on to how you are going to get it, be that an internal quality (self-esteem, peace, creativity, love, kindness) or resolve an external situation (job or career that you love and find fulfilling) or anything else.

What is most important is that you recognize that what you desire is *your* responsibility. In other words, you don't wait around for someone to give it to you. That is not doing your own work. If you want self-esteem, do what is necessary to value who you are. Recognize your great qualities and talents. If you don't have any, do something to build them.

If you don't think of yourself as *valuable*, determine what value means to you and do what is necessary to engulf, embrace, and merge with it. Does this represent providing service, or making a mark, or becoming a hospice nurse, or being kind in every situation? If so, do it.

As you recognize your innate desire and start plugging away at the actions and mindset to move in that direction, be wary of taking on other people's opinions and directives. Most people have loads of ideas of what you should do or be. So, before you accept any of these, weigh them against your own sense of self and choose carefully.

Generally, you will have to count on yourself and not others, because their opinions relate to their work and not yours. Yet, if you discover a tidbit that can work for you, experiment with it until you have proven its worth. If you accept their idea, deal with it until it becomes your idea because, in the long run, you are responsible. Finding your way is *your* work.

Find out what works and what doesn't work to bring you closer to your goal. Listen to your intuition and follow through. If you are like Edison and want to be an inventor, do the research and gain the information you need, then take steps to become an inventor. Be willing to be unlike any other inventor. Inventing will speak to you in a unique way. The same thing is true of being a parent, teacher, artist, nature-lover, engineer, or beach-bum. Whatever you do will be your own unique expression, and it will fit you like a glove. Even if someone helps you along the way, you will still know that you did the work.

Activity: What is your intuitive voice trying to tell you? What ideas are trying to come through for you? What would it take to follow through on them? Which ones are you willing to work with now?

Dark Night of the Soul: Initiation to the Next Phase

It is during our darkest times that we must focus to see the light.
Aristotle Onassis

There is a moment in everyone's life when all the forces of the Universe align to create an instant change. This is not an ordinary change, like moving from one house to the next, or discovering that your treasured friend is not a friend at all. No, this is a time when more is required to you. It is a time of spiritual transformation and, believe it not, it has to be earned.

In the beginning, you may notice a crushing blow to your belief system. Even though you thought you were following all the rules, you discover that the rules you were following were not the right rules. You thought you were being a good girl or boy. It doesn't matter now, because your entire system has to be revised.

It can be a time of devastating depression, self-doubt, and unease about the future. It may appear as a dark period when life seems to come unbidden and without signs of letting up. When your predictable world is shattered and fallen into pieces, you either let the anxiety engulf and destroy you or you step back and examine the fragments to discover what really matters. It is a given that you cannot proceed forward with your current level of competence. You have to face the struggle and embrace it, knowing that it is a sign that you are being tested, that you must offer your grit to keep going.

It is called the *Dark Night of the Soul* for a reason, because all that has come before is now being thrown out. What is left is unknown. It is about transformation and metamorphosis because, in this signature moment, you recognize that your evolution on earth has come with a price, and it is time to pay up, to grow, to release immaturity and to face the gristmill of tough times so that you might be initiated into the next stage.

Why is it described as dark? It is the ego that considers it thus because, at this moment, everything you thought you knew, you now discover you didn't know at all. It was all a presumption. It was following the yellow brick road that you were trained to follow without question, and now it all blew up and the questions remain. *Who am I? Where am I going? What is my life for?* Without a solid basis for living thus far, this dark night might be experienced as a nervous breakdown, as feeling hopelessly lost, or as depression or psychosis. What is really happening is an awakening.

Many books describe this transformational moment. In truth, it is not a bad thing or a bad day. It is a complete reboot of your operating system. At some point in your life, you must leave behind the things of a child and become the person you are meant to be for your life.

Often, we get confused with our upbringing, role models, media presentation, and experiences and believe we have adopted the best of these things to act out a role that is purely fictional. The dark night exposes the necessity of shedding our old skins: values, morals, and beliefs. So that we become a new self.

This transitional phase can seem to come out of the blue, but really, it has been developing and gestating for a while and has finally reached a tipping point.

When our solid, stable world begins to fall apart, it is hard to tell what will happen next, where we are headed, and where we will be when it is over. The truth is that we will never be the same again. We have lost the identity that we had known for years, perhaps our whole life, and the unsteady foundation we have lived with cannot stabilize until we take on a new identity. That is why this event signals the death of the ego. To be sure, the ego does not go down without a fight.

In shamanism, this process indicates that your cognitive systems are updated. That being said, each step forward requires a release of the old self because that is what spiritual revolution is all about. It is a spiritual revolution.

After living a certain way for a long time, people often have a moment of despair, of feeling unsteady, insane. Their world is shaken and yet, there is a liberating aspect in feeling the pain of dissolution as it makes way for newness and the sense that all is not in vain. There is meaning hidden inside of the dark, scary tunnel you have entered. Once the ego and all its make-believe values are dissipated, there is life itself, glistening on the other side.

How you transit through this time determines who you will be for the rest of your life. Do you play a role, or do you become yourself? Are you willing to learn from your experiences and face this death, or do you suffer endlessly as a victim? Is your intelligence ready to break free from the tyranny of your ignorance? How well have you prepared yourself to transcend and transform?

Here are some ways this transition shows itself: Are you beginning to ask yourself questions that seem to have no answers? Why am I here? What is my purpose? What is God and how is He involved?

It might be a time of reevaluating relationships, partnerships, career and life choices, perhaps even sexuality. This transition may be triggered by illness or depression or feeling stuck, or even a desire to jump into something completely new. The world will not necessarily understand, and that is why you must do this for yourself because, in every eventuality, this change will not be deemed proper in a mind of traditional thinking.

The bottom line is that, if you are growing, you are changing and, at some point, it will be important to not only ask the deep questions, but to find the answers. When that happens, it is an indication that you are transforming to a new phase of development and it is good. Fight it if you must, but it will happen anyway, and the more you acknowledge this dark night as an expected and needed transition, the more you will move though it with the least amount of chagrin and most amount of gratitude. You will be ready to step into your next phase. Soon, you will know that you have been blessed!

Activity: What changes are you facing now or in the near future? What actions can you take now to prepare for these changes?

Chapter 5: Imagination and Creativity

Innovation

Genius is nothing more than focusing on a thing.
Abraham-Hicks

Innovation has often been blocked by people lacking imagination. For instance, when Fred Smith outlined his idea for an overnight delivery service, he was told by his Yale professor, "The concept is interesting and well-formed, but in order to earn a better grade than a 'C', it must be feasible." The professor felt that Smith had relied too much on the aviation industry in his design, causing his idea to be flawed and impractical. Smith, fortunately, ignored his teacher's comments and went on to found Federal Express.

When Alexander Bell developed the telephone, most people felt that it wasn't needed on a mass scale. An internal memo at Western Union in 1876 stated, *This "telephone" has too many shortcomings to be seriously considered as a means of communication. The device is inherently of no value to us.*

Great thinkers have always battled negativity. Change, even though it is the pathway for progress, is often resisted. The old guard is too threatened to admit the new guard. Yet, there is value in thinking beyond established norms. To be creative, one must be willing to stand outside what is considered common. Revising and building is not for sissies, for there are many people frightened, jealous and judgmental of innovators.

These folks believe stability is standing still. Yet, the very nature of life is energy in motion. In other words, change is the only constant. Attempting to interfere with it is like trying to stop a moving train by standing in front of it.

A more sensible approach calls for curiosity and an adventurous spirit. Do you need to embrace new ways in your life? Perhaps it is time to become computer-literate, take an economics class, travel abroad, or learn to line dance. Employ your natural sense of adventure to open your mind to new methods. In the process, you will grow and your life will become exciting.

Simplicity

There is more to life than increasing speed.
Mahatma Gandhi

Multitasking is *big* these days. What with computers, the internet, social media, Zoom meetings, e-mail, cell phones, voice mail, and scheduled lives for every family member. It would seem the only way to make it through the day is to multitask. Yes, we live in an age of information explosion, and because of that, we may feel a loss in quality as we divide our attention in dozens of ways. It seems that the number of tasks to be completed and the design of the human brain, don't quite match. Therefore, we must become protective of where we place our attention, protective of what we ask of ourselves as human beings, stuck in a twenty-four-hour-seven-day-a-week world.

Writer Martha Beck offers some wonderful pointers for those who crave a simpler life without losing a sense of purpose. Her first point is to accept that you will not be able to read every bit of mail, respond to every offer, attend every event, and complete every project. Simplification boils down to managing your time by managing your attention.

Secondly, she suggests starting your day with a *clear plan* about where you will be placing your attention. Otherwise, it will get wasted. Prioritizing must be done *before* the day begins because, if you wait, new demands that spontaneously sprout up take over, leaving you overwhelmed and mentally fuzzy.

Plan according to your big picture, or manage your priorities with *eagle-vision.* This means that you consider today's goals in terms of what you want to achieve in the long run. What experiences do you want to have? How do you want your world affected during your time here?

While planning from a big picture, work with *mouse-vision.* Focus directly and completely on the task in front of you. This means to cut out distractions. Not only will mouse-vision eliminate feeling scattered and the accompanying exhaustion, but you will also discover that your concentration improves over time. While you are giving up talking on the cellphone, driving, reading a map, and planning your next meal, what you are gaining is sanity, peace, purpose. and being present.

Leonardo da Vinci said it this way: "Simplicity is the ultimate sophistication."

Taking Risks to See Their Rewards

> *Here's to the crazy ones. The misfits. The rebels. The troublemakers. The round pegs in the square holes. The ones who see things differently. They're not fond of rules. And they have no respect for the status quo. You can quote them, disagree with them, glorify or vilify them. About the only thing you can't do is ignore them. Because they change things. They push the human race forward. And while some may see them as the crazy ones, we see genius. Because the people who are crazy enough to think they can change the world, are the ones who do.*
>
> Rob Siltanen

Many people think you have to be brave to take risks. That is partly true. The other side of risk involves seeing your reward. Gutsy people don't risk for the fun of it, but to achieve an end.

I'm not talking about recklessness, like jumping off cliffs, driving a car too fast, or investing one's life's savings in a questionable stock. I'm referring to more basic experiences, such as interrupting a long, boring conversation, stating an unpopular opinion, being alone, introducing oneself to a stranger, or asserting oneself when one feels misused. These risks, which face us daily, make up the fiber of our lives and speak of our commitment to grow in self-acceptance and love.

Each time you chance expressing yourself openly, you face the possibility of others' rejection. However, you also build self-respect. Respect leads to acceptance, which results in motivation. Who and what do you want to be? Examine the risks necessary to reach that goal. What is it going to take?

Moses took a chance when he left Egypt for the Promised Land. Not only was he responsible for his safety, but the Israelites as well. Moses could have let fear of unknown territory stop him, but he didn't, and the Israelites eventually arrived at their destination, the Promised Land. Moses did not let shortages, enemy attacks or internal unrest interfere.

You don't have to cross the Red Sea to stretch yourself. However, viewing your goal as the promised land will help to motivate you.

Courage is a matter of conviction. You have conviction about things that are important to you. Decide how important your goal is. If it's a high priority, there will be a burning desire and strong determination. Risk is hard when you don't see your benefit. Therefore, take risks with your objective in mind. Fear will dissipate and be replaced with excitement. Build self-respect by walking through your desert of risks, and you will ultimately arrive at your promised land.

Going with the Flow

Have you still got your space? Your soul?
Your own and necessary place,
where your own voices may speak to you, you alone?
Where you may dream? Oh, hold onto it. Don't let it go
Doris Lessing

Drifting along on a sailboat is a great metaphor for flowing along easily in life. There are other comparisons between life and sailing. For instance, when you have your sail set (your goal established), the wind passes through the sails and creates a vacuum (the need for your skills, product or vision.) In sailing, it is the vacuum that pulls the boat forward. Setting the sails properly, serves as an efficient use of wind.

The same can be said of flowing with the winds of time or flowing with the time in which we live. Each period has specific requirements. These needs can be identified and creatively met. A creative person can develop the products that meet the needs of the culture. This is an example of going with the flow or letting the vacuum (the need) pull the boat forward. This brings to mind the saying, "Necessity is the mother of invention."

For instance, after World War II, there was an instant need for affordable housing for the returning soldiers. The people that met this need not only met a real, tangible requirement of the times, but made a lot of money as well. The same can be said of the developers of the light bulb, the airplane, computer, and wash-and-wear clothing. Each was tuned in to the times and found a way to fulfill needs.

There is another position in sailing called the Beam Reach. This is when the sail is perpendicular to the wind and the wind pushes the boat. This is the slowest method to propel the boat forward. Contrast this technique to those who resist life. When everyone is going north, they want to go south. When the whole team is working together, they want to take a solitary approach. (There are always dissenters among us.)

How do you see the needs of this time? Is there a way to set your sails for greater efficiency in order to work with the winds of change and move forward with greater momentum? How might you take advantage of the opportunities at hand?

The Illusion of Age

At which point, folks typically choose one of two paths:
Spend a lifetime lamenting how far from perfect things are.
Or, to one degree or another, roll up their sleeves and pitch in.
Mike Dooley

There is a song called, "What's Love Got to Do with It?" This next segment is a derivation on that theme: "What's Age Got to Do with it?"

Often people equate age with the date on their birth certificate and use that number to determine how they act, live and think. Age becomes an excuse: *When you get to be my age....* Or the reverse: *You're too young to know about that.* They hide behind age, making it the ruling factor in their lives. They make a number more important than who they really are, and in that way, they miss out on life.

The truth is that the number of years you have hung out on the earth could equate to experience, growth, and wisdom. Certainly, a seventy-year-old has had more experience (both wins and losses) than a forty-year-old. It was Presidential Candidate Ronald Reagan, who happened to be in his 70's, who met his opponent in a debate and said, "I hate to pull this card, but I have a lot more experience than my opponent." He was referring to the fact that he had been president of The Screen Actors Guild and governor of California. In his statement, Reagan put age in its proper perspective. The bottom line is: you are in charge of your age. Your age is not in charge of you.

It has been scientifically proven that there is nothing in the body that causes it to age. There are no time-released elements, no alarm clocks set to go off at specific times, causing deterioration. The reason people age in appearance and attitude is because they believe they're *supposed to.* They've programmed themselves and, consequently, their bodies subconsciously to look and act a certain way at respective points in their lives. They believe and accept age as a determining factor, and therefore, it is. These people get old.

Yet, note that there are many other people who have chosen differently. They have not used age or lack of it to determine their success or limit their talent. For instance, at age 42, Ted Williams slammed a home run in his last official time at bat. Another fellow, 20-year-old Mickey Mantle hit 23 home runs in his first full year in the major leagues. (And this was before steroids.)

There was Golda Meir who became Prime Minister of Israel at age 71, and William Pitt II who became Prime Minister of Great Britain at age 24. George Bernard Shaw was 94 when one of his plays was first produced. Mozart was a youngster of seven when his first composition was published. The topper is Benjamin Franklin, who started out as a newspaper columnist at 16 and helped frame the United States Constitution at 81.

It becomes clear that age is irrelevant when you've got a mission. You're never too young or too old to express it. At 99, George Burns said that, "*a happy life is all in having the right attitude and loving your work; getting up in the morning to something you want to do very badly.*"

So, there. You have it. It is up to you. Are you willing to let cultural beliefs dictate what you can and cannot do? Or are you ready to set your own tone and do what you love, leaving age out of the equation?

Challenge Brings Out Inventiveness

Never let the fear of striking out keep you from playing the game.
Babe Ruth

There were two birds flying over the desert: a hummingbird and a vulture. The hummingbird delights in a beautiful cactus flower. The vulture scowls as he locates a carcass. Each find what they are seeking.

We are like these birds. We always find what we seek. It can be a beautiful, fresh opportunity to express creatively and expand our abilities. Or, we can focus on the past, lamenting what was and convincing ourselves that our chances for happiness are gone. Getting stuck in old ways (carcasses) makes it hard to see present possibilities.

Challenges bring out inventiveness in people. Often with a new experience, a kind of paralysis, born of fear, sets in. You can't do things the tried-and-true way because challenges require stretching the mind and imagination. And once you've accepted the opportunity and stretched your mind, you can never go back. Engaging in new opportunities is how you exercise individuality and creativity. Look at your situation and ask yourself how you can *use it* to your advantage, grow with it, find something good in it, create a new strategy.

Often, we feel desolate when confronted with a new experience such as divorce, being between jobs, recovering from illness, experiencing a death. Don't let this limbo period get you down. Free your imagination to perceive the waiting opportunity. Do this by relaxing your mind, accepting your temporary helpless state, and choosing to enjoy it rather than complain.

If you reckon only with the way things used to be or the way they're *supposed* to be, you limit yourself. This is a vulture-attitude dwelling in the past, feeding on death. You can be the optimistic hummingbird, delighting in a beautiful new opportunity (new way or idea), daring to do things differently.

What do you want? For what are you looking? Keep yourself open to possibilities for expansion, for new ways of doing things. Make sure you are not limiting yourself with vulture-attitudes, tying you to the past. Every moment provides challenge. Are you using it to your advantage? Are you finding what you want?

Activity: Is there an impasse in your life right now? Are you experiencing boredom? If so, consider new strategies to accomplish old goals or play with the idea of a new goal. You can make it small to begin with. Take dance lessons, archery, tai chi, or a woodworking class. Do something to shake up your brain neurology. Move your body to Zumba or learn calligraphy. Newness will move you out of your impasse and brighten your day. Don't worry about being the best. Let taking the risk by doing something new be the win. You gain experience and learn to play. That is the win!

Authenticity, A matter of Simplicity

Sing like no one's listening,
Love like you've never been hurt,
Dance like nobody's watching,
And live like it's heaven on earth.
Mark Twain

Authenticity is a matter of simplicity. When one is truly oneself, the trappings of success can seem frivolous and unimportant. The iconic comedian, Will Rogers, experienced great success from his newspaper columns, as well as his stage, radio and movie appearances. His celebrity status garnered him all the money he would ever need, yet he never lost his signature simplicity. He continued to wear the same type clothing as always, a rumpled, general-store style. At the height of his popularity, the furnishings in his dressing room reflected who he was. The furnishings consisted of two old, straight-backed wooden chairs.

His wife Betty wanted to surprise Rogers by redecorating his dressing room. She purchased two soft, comfortable armchairs, a chaise lounge, drapes, lamps and an oriental rug. Everything a celebrity of his caliber might desire. Rogers seemed sincerely appreciative of her thoughtfulness.

Days later, she returned to the dressing room thinking he might be relaxing in one of his new comfortable chairs. Instead, she found him sitting on the floor cross-legged. He commented that he couldn't find any place to sit that suited him. Betty understood. Within a few days, Rogers' dressing room was restored to its original condition. His simple, functional chairs came back. They matched Will Rogers' character. He was not ostentatious and neither were they.

Will Rogers' authenticity was his power and his influence. He stated it best when he said, "I use only one set method in my little gags, and that is to try and keep to the truth." Indeed, he was a master of simple truth.

If and when there are times when you feel pulled this way and that, and you're not sure what you should do or who you should be, remember Will Rogers, for that might bring you back to your authentic self. Once you are centered in your realness, you will have a better sense of what direction is right for you.

Activity: Can you identify one area of your life where you are not fully authentic? If so, question yourself as to why you have chosen to be inauthentic. What are you trying to gain? Is it worth the effort? Are you willing to consider how you might simplify the situation in your own mind so that you can use it as a place to become more authentic?

Suggestion: Admit a failure or hidden fear to a friend or an acquaintance. Notice what happens.

Living in the Abstract

If you knew how each little, fluffy thought or daydream of yours
was tied to the huge, pivotal events of your life,
you'd never again consider any of your thoughts little or fluffy.
Mike Dooley

What is the *abstract*? What it is *not* is the dense, material world. What it is then, is the world of spiritual energy (lightness), that essence of which you are composed and living in and through. Experiencing the abstract means to put your attention on the on-going, consistent energy that never changes. It is your external and internal being.

The easiest way to do this is to go to your heart and feel the subtle energy of love. As you concentrate there, you will find it spreading and taking hold in your entire body and beyond, as though you are a vast bubble of lightness and calm.

To live in the abstract is to live beyond the dense world and, in that way, you are always connected with truth. As mental-spiritual energy, you *can* walk on water. Struggle does not exist. It is in making this your reality that you can be in the world and not of the world.

Mahatma Gandhi could walk into a conflict because he was not part of the conflict. He was above the conflict in knowing the truth: that love is the only reality. Also, he could see as love that all are brothers and sisters, his family. He could see that love was greater than fighting and greater than the strife of the small (egoic) self. So, he called people to a larger reality, knowing that even loss of the dense human self (the container) was an acceptable outcome, because to live in the energy of love was the most important thing. It was the ultimate truth (dharma).

To be untroubled by small people's attachment to right and wrong, choosing who they will love instead of all, and needing the stimulation of five senses to feel alive, is to remain in the reality of love as the only truth. Gandhi radiated love because that was his reality. He lived it and he was joyful. He was also fierce in his knowing and found no difficulty in making what he knew his focus. He recognized a broader, vaster reality, the only one that ultimately counts.

How can you live this reality? To see above each person. To not be taken in by their strife. To bless them with your truth and love, let them be jealous or grieved by it, or welcome it. That part is theirs. Your part is offering it and accepting their decision as theirs.

Chapter 6: Engaging Intuition - Your Source for Divine Guidance

Intellect, Instinct and Intuition

Intuition is seeing with the soul.
Dean Koontz

The body functions spontaneously. The heart beats, cells reproduce, toxins release, and the organs function, all from a perfect design. This is called *instinct. Intuition* is the soul functioning. They are alike in that they carry out their function, yet different in that they function on different levels.

Instinct works in the dense, gross physical body, and intuition is subtle and operates on a soul level. Between the two is yet another element called the mind, which never functions spontaneously. The reason is that the mind garners knowledge and attempts to function intellectually. Knowledge can never be spontaneous.

In the Western world, intellect is honored and touted and yet instinct and intuition are deeper and higher energies, respectively. If you want to understand the full scale of self, it is important to listen to both instinct and intuition and learn how to couple them with the intellect. Intellectual knowledge will always be superseded and replaced in a relatively short space of time, but intuition is timeless.

Intuition, generated from a finer essence, cannot be explained scientifically because the very phenomenon of intuition is unscientific and irrational. In other words, can intuition be reduced to intellect? The answer is No. Intuition is not of the intellect. It is beyond intellect. In fact, it comes from a place where intellect has no awareness. The intellect can *feel it* but cannot explain it, and that is a problem for the intellect, because the intellect wants to disavow anything that cannot be rationally explained or broken down.

Yet, the intellect can *feel* the shift into intuition. There is a gap that indicates something has happened but cannot be explained. Why? Because explanation requires causality and intuition is beyond causality. It emanates from a deeper reality, or level.

Intuition is not related to the intellect at all. Yet, it can penetrate the intellect. Higher reality can penetrate a lower reality, but not vice versa. Thus, your mind can penetrate your body, but your body cannot penetrate the mind. That is why, if you desire higher connection, you must let go of the body and the mind. Neither can penetrate the higher realm of intuition.

Your physical being is gross, heavy and dense. It cannot be lifted into higher consciousness. This is the reason you have to release your body, your identity and your judgmental mind to move into the higher realm of knowing or Light.

You can get stuck and lost in thinking (intellect/chatter) and believe that what cannot be explained intellectually does not exist. That is the belief that keeps you trapped in thinking (not feeling) and disavows mystery, wonder and miracles to come through to you. It is a narrow, closed existence that tethers you to low energy and experience. When you close your mind to wonder, you close your mind to intuitive inspiration, and you live a barren existence. There are no answers.

A purely rational mind that is closed within the boundaries of reason is blocked from entering the space of intuition. However, you can use your intellect without being closed to intuition. You can do this by using reason as an instrument to maintain an open consciousness. When Einstein said, *I know nothing,* he meant, as an intellectual man, he knew nothing. His answers came from a finer realm. The wisdom he aspired to was beyond his intellect, and his desire was to be open and receptive to that higher energy. He wanted to receive it. In that regard, he used intellect as an assist to stay open. He understood that the way of *knowing* was accepting that something had happened that was beyond him. This is the kind of receptivity that helps us understand and move into the gap: the place beyond the body and mind.

The Gap

> *When you want an answer to a question, direct the question to within* you. *Believe and you know that the moment you ask, you are being answered. You don't know how the answer will come, but you will receive it. The answer you receive is the perfect answer for you because you attracted it from within* you.
>
> Mike Dooley

Consider the gap. An easy way to understand what is meant by the gap is to observe your breathing. When you breathe in and before you exhale, you will notice that there is a small gap of time when no breathing is taking place. It is like a tiny rest period. The same is true when you exhale and before you inhale. Notice the space between the two. That is the gap. It is a space of pure openness.

Notice also that there are gaps between thoughts. You can practice placing your attention in this gap (space). As you do this, you will find that you are slipping into a different reality. You will register stillness. Practice staying in the gap for a minute, then ten minutes. In time and with practice, you can move into this gap and expand your consciousness. Slipping into the gap represents an opportunity to experience pure consciousness without the contamination of thinking. In the gap, you are pure being.

Activity: Sit quietly and observe your breathing. You will notice a rhythm to your breathing. Do this for a few breaths until you catch the rhythm. Then, when ready, notice there is a gap or space between the inbreathe and the out breathe, and vice-versa. Just sit and observe this gap. When ready, focus your attention into that gap. It is like slipping through a doorway. Notice the feeling when you do this. There is space and stillness. And what else? Just notice. When you feel ready, you can return your attention to breathing again. Moving into the gap is a wonderful way to still the mind and observe a different kind of reality.

What Is Intuition?

You'll be calm the day you learn to sit alone and do nothing.
Maxime Lagace

I am frequently asked about intuition. What is it? How do I know if I am operating from intuition? Is it real or something I have made up? Great questions! Let's explore the answers.

As an intuitive counselor and akashic-record reader, I rely on my intuition in both business and personal life. I start my day with meditation. As the day unfolds, I check my every decision to make sure it is aligned with highest energy. That is a most important function of intuition, to keep you on track and connected to your spiritual Source.

Because intuition is your guide to Highest Intelligence, you must ask the question: *Would I rather be given advice from my Highest Self or my ego?* The ego is reactionary, small, jaded, and self-protective. Therefore, it does not take in the full picture of what is going on. Intuition has no such limitation. Cultivating and strengthening your intuitive voice is one of the most important things you will ever do. It will make your life easier, less stressful, and simpler. I think of it as my spiritual aid in getting me to my destination as the crow flies, the shortest path.

As a professional, I depend on my still small voice for insights and instructions in every situation. When I work with clients, I am guided to the right energy, symbols and scenarios that supply the most meaning and impact for them. The messages that come through my intuitive channel are relatable, practical, and provide my clients the clearest way to accomplish what is needed, and I mean *as the crow flies*.

The truth is that we live on many levels. The physical/material world happens to be the heaviest (densest), energetically. The finer realms, where intuition resides, are clear, insightful and packed with wisdom. By following your intuition, you will discover ways to heal and to express your highest energy, passions and goals.

As Dean Koontz instructs, intuition is seeing with the soul. That means you shift your attention from the five physical senses and focus on the deep feeling that comes through as intuition. We call it the still small voice because it is subtle and presented as knowing. You just *KNOW*!

Of course, the more you pay heed to intuitive feelings, the stronger they become. Strengthening your intuition is very much like exercising a muscle. The more you work the muscle, the stronger it gets. You can do the same with your intuitive "muscle."

You might notice intuition if and when you are in a conflict situation and you feel prodded to do or say something. It informs you if something is right or wrong for you, and even may offer insights about situations and relationships. It could come in a flash. Yet again, if cultivated, you can hear it as your primary guidance.

You are often tuned to it when quiet and heart-focused. This may require you to shut off your analytical intelligence or ego and move into feeling. When you run through life letting your intellect (head) lead the way, living by rigid rules and forced decisions, you are continually distracted by external noise (mental chatter) and unable to listen deeply. The reason for this is that you are making the external world your reality.

The material world is loud, dramatic and demanding. If that is your total reality, you will find it difficult to cultivate the deep inner listening necessary to access inner wisdom. This condition can be eradicated by filtering in daily quiet time. It is a choice. Do you want chaos and noise or stillness and connection?

Hence, to connect to inner knowing, you must step away from the drama of the physical world. Turn off the television and phone and get quiet. Take a break. Stop. Place your attention on the heart, sit quietly, consciously breathe, and listen. Begin with five minutes a day. This allotted time will naturally expand as you develop the mental discipline to manage stillness.

Is It Real or Are You Making It Up?

The keenness of our vision depends not on how much we can see, but on how much we feel.
Helen Keller

There are studies that illustrate the benefits of intuition. A 2015 study presented in the "Journal of Positive Psychology" indicates that intuition is particularly beneficial when a person is stressed or under pressure. It states that intuitive processes often lead to conclusions of higher value than rational, analytic methods of reasoning.

A "Forbes" article states that scientists and researchers have proven that intuition is the highest form of intelligence. It is noted that gut-feelings, hunches, or the still small voice of intuition contain power, insight and truth. In fact, it offers much more insight than the data available in the outside world.

You can use intellect and intuition together. Use reason to back up intuition in much the way that Einstein did. He would intuit a premise (the speed of light or the law of relativity) and then go to work with his logical mind to find the formulas to back up his intuitive insight.

Elmer Gates was an inventor that used intuition whenever he got stuck on one of his projects. His method was to sit in a darkened, quiet room and focus on the issue at hand and wait. Eventually, he would receive the information he needed to resolve the problem. Ideas showed up as potentials, a new way to proceed. For years, Gates worked for corporations and businesses by sitting and listening to unlock the key to pressing issues. Ultimately, his methods worked and he proved to be a master inventor.

Another prolific inventor, Thomas Edison, also knowingly used intuition. When he had exhausted his ideas regarding a project he was working on, he would purposely lie down on the cot in his laboratory and take a nap. Before he rested, he programmed his mind to provide solutions to his dilemma upon awakening. His method was to hold a steel ball or object in his hand as he rested. When he fell asleep, his hand relaxed and the object fell to the floor and woke him up. Whatever was in his mind as he awakened was his answer. His method obviously worked. He filed over 200 patents during his career.

Thus, there are various ways one can move into the subtle realm of intuition. The easiest way to cultivate or build an intuitive channel is by utilizing daily quiet time.

What's the Benefit?

The time Steve Jobs procrastinated and pondered the possibilities was time well spent, letting more divergent ideas emerge.
Adam Grant, Wharton Professor

The beautiful thing about intuition is that it never lies or steers you in the wrong direction. When you dwell in the intuitive mind, you develop clarity, a big-picture approach to life. Intuition displaces fear with love. It is vitally important to never make a decision out of fear or anger because it will lead to results that may seem appropriate at the time but are ultimately disastrous, because they are reactionary and do not take in the long view of a situation. Be careful of fear. It drowns out intuition and blocks forward movement. It is restrictive, confining and shortsighted.

Whereas fear constricts and creates anxiety, love is expansive. You may get an intuitive *don't-do-it* signal, but the energy around that message is lighter and more perceptive than the energy of fear. As you observe, intuition *feels* right. There is a sense of clarity and knowing that goes with it.

When connected intuitively, you naturally feel calm. Peace is indicative of truth. Conclusions always come easier when operating from this higher realm. Even with a *don't-do-it* or *this-is-a-bad-idea* message, there is still a sense of ease or rightness. The fact is, intuition never goes against your desire. On the contrary, it supports and moves you toward it. And clear thinking always produces confidence.

How Does It Come Through to You?

The next message you need is always right where you are.
Ram Dass

There are a variety of ways that your inner voice can speak to you. Feelings are important. Notice the feeling. A sense of peace or repulsion conveys choices. A sense of lightness signals you know you are on the right path. When feeling constructed or repulsed, you know you are not. Your body does not know how to lie, and you will be guided when you listen to it.

Dreams, day or night, are another way to receive messages. Dealing with symbolism of dreams helps you understand the urges coming through. Also, always note the feeling portrayed in a dream. It unerringly reflects that either fear or love is dominant in your thinking.

Symbolism is important. For instance, a person who dreams of being a superhero most likely will become one. Perhaps not with a cape and laser gun, but still a superhero. That person may discover a new way to accomplish a purpose, heal an illness, rocket to space, or develop a higher technology.

Recently, I had a client who dreamed of earthquakes, floods and disaster. She knew she must leave her job because it was having a negative effect on her. Another client met her beautiful, unconditionally loving mother in her dreams and was told that she is doing everything as she should and to continue. Both understood that they were being guided.

Intuition also shows up as symbolism in your waking life. When I see ambulances, police cars and fire trucks, I am alerted to be attentive to what I am doing, to stay grounded, be aware. You may see a word that shows up everywhere you go, *Slow Down*, or an animal, like a deer, which instructs you to be gentle (often this means with yourself). You may see a hawk, which bears the message to take the long view. Indeed, the Universe communicates through intuition in many ways.

Build Your Intuition Connection

The spiritual life does not remove us from the world
but leads us deeper into it.
Henri J M Nouwen

Here are some practices that will help you build a connection to intuition:

1) G*et in touch with your authentic self.*

Through our lives, we have buried and hidden our true selves under personalities and behavioral roles in order to follow the rules, stay safe, and be acceptable. We have paid a huge price for this because we end up living in the dense world of ego instead of the deeper reality of truth. In playing it safe, we have constructed blocks, psychological beliefs that keep us from recognizing our innate gifts and purpose. We must drop these false personas and get honest.

You know what you love to do, how you love to express, and contrarily, the things you find distasteful. These preferences have been evident from the time you were a small child. If possible, work with someone who can help you peel away the layers of erroneous beliefs to free your spirit and make the connection with your true self. By living a life of honesty, your intuition will get stronger and louder.

Getting clear on who you truly are as a spiritual being will help you let go of the past and build a foundation of self-love. This is an essential shift because intuition resides in love. If you disdain yourself, you stay boxed in fear and closed-mindedness. Your Higher Self, the source of intuition, is pure love. Loving yourself stabilizes your connection to intuition. It is mandatory.

Self-love can be the ultimate life lesson. Learning to accept yourself, warts and all, flaws and mistakes, without judgment or self-denigration, the more you live in the highest vibrational reality. When judgment dissolves, Intuition thrives.

2) *An important practice is to learn to be still.*

Creating space to be quiet, meditate, breathe and enjoy nature, pays dividends. Stillness allows you to connect with your heart, gut, inner hunches or intuitive voice. With a *stillness* practice, intuition strengthens day-by-day. Additionally, let go of negative or chaotic situations and relationships. They are draining and keep you stuck. Also remove distractions and clutter. This will help to quiet mental chatter and drama. Clutter reflects a cluttered mind. Within this reclaimed space, your intuition will grow stronger.

3) *Pay attention to your physical body to notice feelings that come up for you.*

Perhaps you feel uneasy about a person or situation. Or you may feel a strong *Yes.* Whatever you are feeling, take time to explore it. Ask questions to gain clarity. With practice, it becomes obvious. Is this feeling coming from inner knowing or fear? Exploration of this type develops discernment.

4) *Develop listening through channeled writing.*

Write a question on a piece of paper, take a few deep breaths, clear your mind, and write. You can wait for the words to start flowing, or you can make circles on the paper until they surface. Once the words come, start writing. Don't filter or concern yourself with spelling, grammar, sentence structure, or making sense of it. Just keep writing until the words play out. Trust the process. Don't judge it. Your intuition is a tool, focused on helping you live your highest life. Often the answers that come through are not the ones you think you want. But that goes to trust. Being honest is imperative to developing a strong relationship with your intuition.

As you gain strength at trusting your inner voice, making choices gets easier because you are mentally clear. Decisions come faster and are aligned with what is best for you. Anxiety is minimized because you no longer agonize or let your rational/intellectual mind dominate. Because you are in attunement with your Higher Mind, instant feedback becomes your method, and it offers the best option for you.

5) *Becoming familiar and comfortable with your intuitive voice makes it vastly easier to put it into practice.*

For instance, let's say you are looking to change jobs. You might start thinking about each job opportunity you are considering. You explore the fears, dreams and visions associated with each one. What do you want your work environment to feel like? As you imagine the various activities of the job, how do they feel? Does it feel enlivening or heavy? Are you learning something important? Does it align with your career goals? You need to write these feelings down to get the full picture. Again, feelings give rise to inner truth. The important thing is to pay attention and do not dismiss them.

By asking questions, you define the issue. What do you want to get clear about? With career, for instance, determine this and you will be ready for potential solutions. Should you stay or go? And if you go, what option is best for you? Working for another company? Being self-employed? Being a full-time employee or a contract-based employee? Starting a different career? Doing something completely new?

Write down various options and let your intuition guide you to what feels best. What feelings show up in your body? The body is a great barometer of truth because it does not know how to lie. It will always give honest feedback. You can mentally rationalize, but your body cannot. What do you feel? Relaxed, relieved, or peaceful? Then your answer is probably *Yes*. Or does your body feel tense, anxious or distressed? If so, the solution you are considering is not the right one or your timing may be off.

If you are still unsure, imagine going forward, implementing each possibility. With your imagination engaged, you will get immediate intuitive feedback. By imaging the new scenario, the body will actually feel it because it does not know the difference between a real or an imagined experience. Visualize doing solution one. Move into it. How do you feel with each step? Are you fearful yet excited? Or do you feel dread and repulsion? Each feeling is an intuitive guide. Go through each possibility and you will know what is best.

Take time to differentiate if your reactions are grounded in fear or love. Remember, fear feels heavy and restrictive. If you notice that feeling, give yourself time to contemplate what you are afraid of. In other words, explore the fear. It is possible that the initial fear is not the real fear. By getting to know your fear, you also learn more about yourself. All fear is irrational. Yet, exploring it may help you let it go. To say this differently, the only valid fear is when your life is endangered, like being chased by a bear. More than likely, the fear you feel is a remnant from the past and not really relevant to your situation.

Other fears might relate to being embarrassed or failing at a task or someone not liking you. These are the fears that keep you stuck and must be acted on. We are human beings having a learning experience. Listening to your intuition will help you learn and grow. Life is a process, not a destination. When it feels right, walk through the fear and face it head-on. As you do this, you will become free. Fear can never hook you again. You have defeated it.

As you use these tools, you will create a strong connection to your higher mind and intuition. Your life will flow more easily. You will have more clarity and joy.

Intuition Goes Beyond Intellect

Within you there is a stillness and a sanctuary
to which you can retreat at any time and be yourself.
Hermann Hesse

Our Western Culture, in particular, has glorified thinking and intellectual attainment to the total dismissal of the higher state of intuition. Now, it is time to reverse this conclusion.

It is well known that the great scientist, Marie Curie, who first understood atomic energy, received the formula she sought in a dream. After days of frustrated effort coming up dry, she finally yielded to fatigue and went to bed. During the night, she woke up with a dream wherein the formula she sought was presented. She woke up well enough to write down the formula and then went back to sleep. In the morning, she looked at her note pad and saw the formula. She checked it out in her laboratory and found that it was the exact formula she needed, the answer to her quest to understand atomic energy. As a result, Curie won a Nobel Prize for discovering atomic energy.

The great scientist, Albert Einstein, was well aware of intuition and used it effectively in his work. He said, *Imagination is more important than knowledge. Knowledge is limited. Imagination encircles the world.* He used his imagination as he rode a light beam into space. It was his use of imagination that led him to understand the law of relativity. It came to him intuitively. He let intuition lead the way. He followed this knowing with logic (intellect) to create his formulas. He understood that the higher cannot be reduced to the lower, and so he aspired to the highest levels of intuition to draw into his awareness the answers he sought.

Known and Unknown

Being at ease with not knowing is crucial for answers to come to you.
Eckhart Tolle

Intuition happens to you, without any physical causality. Without following a logical path of what came before, it shows up. If there was an intellectual process to intuition, you could develop it, like tuning to a particular station on the radio. But it is not an intellectual process. The best way to have control over intuition or learn how to tune at will, is to cultivate deep curiosity, wonder and appreciation for all things natural. In fact, by engaging in deep curiosity and wonder, you are moving into a wide energetic spectrum of consciousness, a vast space that yields to intuitive awareness. You would be developing stillness. At that point, you would be able to *tune in* as needed.

According to logic, there are two realms of existence: the known and the unknown. The unknown implies that which is not yet known but may someday be known. On the other hand, mysticism would indicate that there are three realms: the known, the unknown, and the unknowable. The unknowable refers to that which can never be known. As it says in the Tao, *If you can define it, it is not the Tao*. This means that the Universe is vast, deep and profound, and the dense intellectual equipment of man will never be able to penetrate it or know it. Also, the second you name something, you limit it. The nature of the Tao, or God, or the Universe, is unlimited. It cannot be limited.

The intellect is involved with the known and the unknown, but not the unknowable. Intuition works with the unknowable (that which cannot be known). The unknowable will always exist as the unknowable. It is the realm of intuition. That is why, when you are stuck in a formula or invention, as with Albert Einstein or Marie Curie, you must go to the unknowable for your answer. You might say you can feel it and maybe hear it, but you cannot understand it or break it down into logical little puzzle pieces. This sounds nonsensical, but in essence, it means that the Tao cannot be understood by our physical senses and intellect. The unknowable is the mystery and beauty of life. It is the unknowable that provides life's deepest meaning.

Reason is an effort to know the unknown
And intuition is the happening of the unknowable.
To penetrate the unknowable is possible,
But to explain it is not.
The feeling is possible, the explanation is not.
Osho

We Live in Two Worlds

When you connect to the silence within you,
that is when you can make sense of the disturbance going on around you.
Stephen Richards

We live in two worlds, an inner world and an outer world. The outer world or outer self looks out at the earth and makes believe it is real, believes that the stories we have been told and that we have told ourselves contain the truth, that it matters if someone likes you or doesn't, that a particular fantasy has anything to do with who you are. This outer focused self gets so enamored with the drama, twists, and turns of earth life, you become depressed and try to control everything: things, events and people. You end up frustrated because your efforts fail. This outer self (ego/personality) feels tremendous loss because its truest ambition is to be loved. That equates to being approved of, which means you must do everything right or at least *appear* successful. It ends up a crazy game.

The illusion is that this outer self (ego) can achieve that sense of being loved through other people. So, it scavenges to find those outer resources: people to love them. Later, when it becomes clear that the other person is doing the same thing, scavenging for love, the whole thing falls apart.

The pinnacle that these relationships balance on is an agreement to love and accept each other, flaws and all. This is where growth can take place, for you can achieve an honest balance to love and be loved. Ultimately, this is the way you learn to give and receive unconditionally. It can be the greatest breakthrough of your life, your reason for existing. And the beauty of it is that, learning to love unconditionally, is not dependent on what anyone else thinks and does.

The other part of self, which happens to be the greater self, kind of like the bulk of the iceberg beneath the surface of the tiny out-cropping of the visible iceberg, is your inner self. The inner self is ever-calm and objective. It *sees* and *hears* beyond the clattering and noise of the outer world. *It is the observer.* It can be in the world but not of the world. It can do this because it is not attached to the stories that sweep the news, or the latest calamity: *the world is coming to an end, you are vulnerable to the latest germ showing up on radar, the bad guys are going to get you*, etc.

Your inner world is your true self. It knows love. You might say that it *is* love. It also understands that life is made up of experiences, and we get to choose what we want to do with them. Many people, because they have bought into the earth drama, forget to stay connected with their inner world. They have nervous breakdowns or go crazy. Nevertheless, at any time, you can reconnect with your inner world, your center, the place of peace.

It would seem that with the havoc of change occurring in the world, connecting to your inner world of stillness and peace might be a really terrific idea.

So, how do you do that? Be aware that, more than likely, this *refocus* will take time and practice. This is particularly true because there is a societal addiction to drama. There are those who find it entertaining and love the negative stimulation, something to talk about. They are entranced by it. Or they feel the way to have community is to connect with all the drama. It is like a fix for a drug addict. So, they tune into the news or call their friends and share victim stories. Ah, they are back into the outer world of frenzy and noise. It might seem more fun than peace and quiet, but the outcome is not fun. It's nervousness, worry, anxiety, ill-health.

There is a growing group of folks who clamor for something bigger, more joyful, loving and kind. Those are the ones that break the addiction. They gladly connect to the heart and feel the love that ever-radiates out through the heart into their bodies and lives.

If you are one of those, start by becoming an observer. Begin with your breath. Watch it come in as you inhale and go out as you exhale. Notice the rhythm of the breath and then observe how your mind begins to still as you breathe. Do this conscious breathing for ten minutes until you are fully into observer mode. If you forget and get distracted, pull back to the world of effects, gently return your attention to mindful breathing.

The next step is to stay calm as you observe the world. It starts with people. Observe behaviors and belief systems. Notice how each thought creates some kind of reaction: excitement, creativity, movement, or whatever. Each thought will bring a person up (elevate) or down (depress or deplete). Notice, also, that when a thought is altered, it can have a completely different effect. Someone may be angry about a seeming slight. Then that person decides to let it go and the energy lightens.

As you recognize yourself more and more as *the observer*, you will take this newfound ability into yourself and observe your own thoughts, motives, desires and needs. You will also find that you can do a *change on demand* and re-route your energy right back to your center.

For example, the store clerk may be feeling pressured and expresses it in rudeness. You may react to this affront and decide it means something about you. You fall back into the old story: *I'm not good enough. No one likes me. I have lots of flaws. I am without value, blah, blah, blah.* Then, because you observe yourself going off the rails, you decide to halt the negative chatter and let the whole thing go. You drop the reaction. You drop your judgment of the event, your interpretation of what the store clerk is doing or saying. You remember that you are your inner self and, consequently, good, kind, loveable and ingenious. Because you have chosen to move back to your center, your true self, you can walk on in life unscathed and ready for the next adventure. You will experience the next one as your true self in a state of calm and discovery.

Yes, it is worth the effort to change!

Keep Your Energy High (Raise Your Vibration)

He who is filled with love is filled with God himself.
Augustine of Hippo

Someone mentioned that she did not understand how you could alter an event or situation by raising your energy, by choosing to feel happy, peaceful and loving. I told her that she or anyone else could easily ascertain how this is accomplished. I offered a simple suggestion involving an unpretentious act of walking into a gas station to pay the bill and smiling at the station attendant.

Her face brightened at this idea. "Yes, I have done this and said to that person, 'I hope you have a great day.' I have seen the positive effect my smile and demeanor had on him."

I replied, "Then you understand how easy it is to alter the energy of a situation."

One small act, done with intention, can make any circumstance better. You can go to a party with the idea of contributing to everyone else's comfort and fun and, immediately, your attention is removed from your needs and focused on helping others. And guess what? You feel better. Or you can go to work intending to make your workplace more pleasant and positive. Your intention leads you to smile and wait on customers graciously, treat people with kindness, answer the phone enthusiastically, view vendors as a resource rather than an annoyance, and take pride in what you do.

Raising your energy is not a miraculous thing. It can be accomplished with the simplest intention. And when it is, the giver and the receiver both benefit.

If you get trapped in a negative mindset, change your focus to doing something nice for another person. The act and intention not only releases negativity but sets you on a path of happiness. You feel joyful because it is through giving that a person begins to understand how much he has to offer. As you realize that you have gifts to give, you have a true awareness of value: Self-Value! Truth: When you keep your energy high, your channel to highest inspiration, intuition and love opens.

Activity: Give positivity, love, a smile, a greeting, something away today. Do it again tomorrow and the next day. Notice how you feel.

High Vibrational Energy Heals Mind and Body

You must find the place inside yourself where nothing is impossible.
Deepak Chopra

There are simple and profound healing practices that can be used at any time and with any condition, be it mind, body or spirit. In Baird T Spalding's books, *The Lives and Teachings of the Masters of the Far East,* there is a treasure-trove of wisdom. Much of it relates to shifting awareness and healing.

In his book series, Spalding refers to a healing temple that exists in the Far East as a material structure. It is an exquisite edifice that, upon entering, evokes healing to all who attend. An interesting fact is that there exists an exact replica of this healing structure within each person. It is called the Christ-Mind, and it works in exactly the same way as the bricks and mortar Eastern structure.

Our internal healing structure, the Christ-Mind (or Higher Mind), is also available at all times. Both temples represent the ideal of perfect alignment with our internal Christ-Self: love.

In the highest energy of the Christ-Mind, you find perfect harmonious vibrations. In either temple, external or internal, the temple takes on, over time, this highest vibratory quality because, in its continued use, it allows *nothing of an inharmonious nature to become a part of it.* You might say that a definite thought condition has been established for such a long time that the temple has absorbed it. Unless the thought you attempt to give out is equal to the vibratory quality of the temple, it cannot be brought forth into worlds. It cannot be manifested. It has to match resonance.

According to Spalding, the definite thought condition has been established in that temple. The whole structure has taken it on, merged with it. Unless the thought one attempts to give out is equal to the vibrations of the temple, it cannot be brought forth or manifested. In the same way, as you train your mind-temple to respond to a higher influence, a lower vibration may attempt to impinge, but it is immediately thrown back and rejected.

Consider training your mind-body temple to respond to a high vibratory frequency: positive possibility, love, forgiveness, kindness, generosity. Keep at it for an extended period, like days, months or years, to the point where you have become so accustomed and confirmed in this high vibration that, if or when a lower frequency, like hate, anger, resentment or guilt, attempts to invade, it is immediately tossed out. Consider conditioning your mind in this way. Refuse negativity, anger, guilt, etc. Allow loving, kind, compassionate, positive thought to take hold.

This is exactly what happens when you send forth *only harmonious words,* when you *refuse to judge others,* when you *reach out with the highest intentions and kindness.* Or, take it further. If your body is trained to respond to a high influence, a lower vibrational energy may not enter. Your automatic response is to reject it, throw it out. As a result, your body has the strongest possibility of existing in vibrancy: health.

We must accomplish this task from within because everything is within. Bringing it forth as our automatic expression requires accepting that it is there, that it is completed, and that it is who we have chosen to be.

Suggestion: meditate on this theme or subject and allow the idea of perfect health in mind, body and soul, to become a dominant knowing.

Do you have any ideas as to what to release from your thoughts, beliefs and actions? No more toxic thoughts or actions. Fear, hate, animosity, resentment, jealousy and greed most go. In their place, you build the energy of love, acceptance, kindness, joy and generosity that transfers to the body and assumes the condition of health. You can do that today.

Referencing the temple and all healing work in Spalding's books, the temple is within you. It is a place of high energy. The way you access it is by holding a mental idealized picture of perfect health and vitality. As you do this, you are assuming responsibility for directing energy to the body as a revitalized organ of health, rather than looking to the external world for healing.

By taking the attitude that we know these things exist and work with them, healing does takes place. If we accept these conditions, we bring them forth and can live at one with them in perfect alignment and harmony. At this point, negativity is defused and tossed out. We are living as our harmonious Christ-Selves.

Activity: Keep a journal and set an intention in the morning to speak and act positively in all situations. At night, go through your day and note any time when you strayed from your intention. Imprint these deviations so that, as you set your next day's intention, you will remain on course. With mindfulness and awareness, you can raise your energy and vibration and take on a highly functional state of healing and kindness. In that way, your temple has reverted to its divine state.

Love is Your Core

Being fully present to what is –
without judging or evaluating or wanting something different –
is the most basic act of love.
C. W. Huntington, Jr., *The Miracle of the Ordinary*

The Universe is filled with energy. The great physicist, Albert Einstein, referred to this energy as the Unified Field. He said that it is everywhere and in everything. In fact, all things and people are composed of this energy. That is to say that, if we were to take a high-powered microscope and look deep into a chair, a book, a car, or a physical body, we would discover that at its core, at a sub-atomic level, we would find this energy, this Unified Field. That is also to say that, since we are all composed of this energy and it is within us, all around us, and everywhere, we are connected, one to the other, by It. It is like an ocean of energy in which we live, breathe and have our being.

Currently scientists are calling this energy the Holographic Field or the Quantum Field. Some even refer to it as God or the Universe.

If we were to examine this field of energy sub-atomically, it would appear as light. Therefore, all material and non-material substance (air, radio waves, electricity, microwaves) have the same basis, light. Light is the finest substance or essence of energy.

Taking this premise a bit further, the essence of light is love. Hence, light and love (impersonal, non-romantic love that is) are the same thing. At our core, we are love. The Bible states it as, *God is love.* Can we, therefore, conclude that at our core lies divinity? Can it also follow that the light that emanates from babies, before they have been domesticated, is love? For sure, it feels that way. In fact, that same light and love is magnetic and attractive in an active kind of way. Babies certainly attract people and attention. Therefore, in our basic structure, we are magnetic and attractive. That is the nature of energy.

How then did we lose our awareness of our divine nature and, more importantly, how can we return to it?

Because love is magnetic, it is *the glue of the Universe.* It holds everything together in this one field of energy. It certainly is the glue of friendship and family.

We might compare the love that we have within to the light of the sun. It is brilliant and pure. It radiates constantly to all beings, unconditionally and without judgment. The sun pours its light on the rich and poor, the good and not so good. If we draw an analogy from the radiant sun, and revert back to our original state of divinity, our template or directive is to radiate our love and light to all beings without condition or judgment. If we pretend to love in any other way, it is not really love.

The light of the sun radiates on the rich and poor, the good and bad, and the positive and negative, without discrimination. Studying this analogy helps us understand the concept of universal love. It doesn't request that we be anything but who we are. It doesn't require straight A's on your report card, that you have great hair, or that you win popularity contests. It loves the people in the ghetto, the janitor and the CEO, equally.

As babies, we loved freely. Did we forget? As adults we must learn to love freely again. Love draws together, unites and bonds all things: the wife and husband, the parent and child, friend to friend, one culture to another, and so on. Love expands who we are. Expressing love allows us to be our natural selves.

Somewhere along the way, during our progression from infancy to adulthood, we were taught to withhold love. We were taught to distrust and we developed conditionality. That is when we became bottled up and restricted. This restriction shows itself in our bodies as ill-health or dis-ease.

We told ourselves that we can't love someone if that person doesn't look like us, or have the same beliefs, or wear the same kind of clothes, or speak the same language. When we convinced ourselves of the validity of these conditions, we began to lose touch with our radiance. We closed down a bit. We began to shrink our Light. It is still present, but we are looking the other way. We are looking out there instead of in here, in the heart. By doing that, we make our conditionality real and relevant.

Love is expansive. Certainly, you can feel this when you love someone or something. As expansive energy, it increases whatever you focus on. It also increases you. That which you love increases. Examples: People who love music create and express beautiful music, lots of it. When you love your work, you increase your creativity and expressiveness in your work and you are successful. When you love the money you have, it increases. (Love money for what it can supply you, not make it your God.) Love your friendships and you have more.

On the contrary, when you resist, constrict, judge and avoid these things, you diminish what you have and you lose energy and potential. This is true with work, expression, friendship, money, success, everything. What you resist, you diminish yourself and all that is around you.

Do you want to expand the love you radiate? Start with self-love. That is where restriction first happens. We forget to love, appreciate and accept ourselves.

It is literally impossible to love others until you have mastered the art of loving yourself. If you restrict love to yourself, you will also restrict your flow of love to others. Contrarily, as you increase self-love, you open your channel of love, which radiates to all in your life.

Complete the following worksheet to learn how to love yourself. Here are questions that can help you identify your level of self-love and offer hints on how to expand it.

Activity:

List behaviors that show self-love. Examples: daily exercise, regular quiet time, eating nutritious food, massages, meditation, time spent nurturing friends, bubble baths, reading your favorite book, speaking kindly to yourself, anything that nurtures you.

List behaviors that diminish self-love (self-effacing behaviors). Examples: over-work, verbal put downs, eating on the run, never saying "No," continued relationships with toxic people.

Circle the self-loving and non-self-loving behaviors that you practice. Add more if they apply.

Of the non-self-loving behaviors, which are you willing to release or change?

What do you do to show caring toward three people close to you?

Name three things you are doing for achievement in your life now.

List five things that you do for fun.

Create a Self-Contract. List behaviors and actions you are committing to for the sole purpose of increasing self-love. Create a new contract each week. This week I will:

Chapter 7: Wisdom

Feel God

Happy people build their inner world;
unhappy people blame their outer world.
Dalai Lama

The simple truth is that we are composed of the one energy that exists in the world, the Quantum Field, which also happens to be the energy of God. As most people grew up, they were taught that God is a mythical being that lives in heaven and is not particularly accessible. But that is not true. God is not an old man sitting in a heavenly chair, throwing thunder bolts at people, and conniving ways to punish them. God is a presence *hidden* inside you and quite accessible, particularly when you focus on your heart and become quiet.

You can feel God. It is an internal rhythmic energy of peace. The trick is to turn inward. Take your attention away from the external, material world and focus inside to the stillness.

There are a variety of ways to make this connection or feel this energy, and the best one is to just be quiet. Stillness is a matter of mental training that allows you to experience the peaceful energy that is God.

Krishnamurti describes the process like this: *The moment you have in your heart this extraordinary thing called love and feel the depth, the delight, the ecstasy of it, you will discover that for you, the world is transformed.*

In this book, in the section called, "The Gap," a technique is offered to assist you in moving into the still presence of God. As you practice being quiet, you will strengthen your brain neurology to be able to spend longer and longer periods in this stillness. It may seem hard in the beginning for two reasons, your brain is not practiced at being still for very long and your mind has been trained to be easily distracted. Yet, in time and with practice, these challenges can be overcome. It takes training.

While you are developing stillness, be alert and listen. It is not that you are listening for a particular sound. What you are listening for is the stillness of the Presence of God. As you perfect the practice, your inner sense will expand and you will come to *Know*. The Bible states, *Be still and know that I AM God.*

Another understanding that helps you move deeper into the feeling of God is to feel love. Love and God are the same. In this practice, you are feeling a new depth of love. It is what Krishnamurti and other masters express as ecstasy. The best way to approach this greater depth is to feel God as love until your understanding of love deepens and you become love.

It is true that, whatever you occupy your mind with, you become. That means that, if you spend all your time feeling jealous of other people, you become jealousy. Likewise, if you are consumed with anger, you become anger.

In your desired scenario, occupy your mind with love. Love, for no other reason than it feels good. It lifts your spirit, it transforms your life, it is your natural expression, and it is your pathway to God.

You are designed to radiate love. Radiating love is the same as *giving* love. If you were to shift into a *getting* mode, you reverse the natural current of energy in your body. This is not to say that you are not allowed to receive love, because that is part of the natural cycle of giving and receiving, and there is balance in that. Receiving love and getting love are two different things. Receiving is receptive and getting is aggressive.

It takes courage to go deep inside and love because it is not the general mode of our culture. Yet, when you go deep into any emotion or feeling, only that emotion remains. The personal you ceases to exist. That is total giving. You may even feel a moment of *you* disappearing. But it is only the ego you that ceases to exist.

As you intensely focus on love, you may feel the personal, egoic self-disappearing for longer periods. In this way, you are mastering the art of being love. As you do this, you lose your dependency on the external world. It doesn't mean that you will physically disappear or die. It means that you will live more fully in a deeper state of your True Self. You will experience true freedom and ecstasy.

Activity: Start by spending ten minutes a day feeling love. You can begin by thinking of someone or something that you truly love. This will be a trigger for you. After you have spent a week using this trigger, feel love more deeply. You can do this by feeling love for nature or for the starry sky. Then go deeper, feel love as an energy. Then feel the energy of love as you encounter each person in your world. Soon you will ignore other emotions that distract you because the dynamic energy of love is so magnetic and powerful. You will choose to stay in that feeling and you will become love.

Strengthen Your Heart Center

When you connect to the silence within you,
that is when you can make sense of the disturbance going on around you.
Stephen Richards

The organ of the heart represents an energy center known as the Heart Center. It is the place where pure love is expressed. Often, when people take things personally or feel offended or hurt, they shut down this center. They might continue to seek love and attention from others, always looking to the outer for their source of love, but they are *not giving love,* and that is their mistake because love expands in the giving of it. If you make giving love (affirmation, smiles, appreciation, kindness, compassion) your mission, your heart expands, which means you will have more and more love to give. You will have less and less dependency on the world. You will have discovered a new world: the one inside of you.

Start by giving love in every situation. What would love do in this situation? Forgive, console, offer assistance, smile, try to understand, show compassion, be kind? Instead of fretting about your own needs, tend to others' needs. Do it for five minutes, an hour, a full day. Soon you will glow with love and your heart will be strong.

Open yourself to adjust the concept of God to a kind, open, loving heart or hearth, a nurturing warmth, an energy. Receive the recognition that your spiritual relationship is present without effort. You may have to get used to an idea that you don't have to work at this. It is a matter of being receptive, soft and open.

To practice, mimic the energy of God. Align with it. Do this by relaxing and noticing the rhythm of your body. Go into a park or natural area and observe the quiet rhythm of nature, the wind as it blows through the trees, the animals as they scurry, the birds as they dig for worms. There is a rhythm. Feel it and give yourself to it. Sit with it. Breathe with it. Love it!

By merging with this rhythm, you open to Spirit. Let your mind relax and breathe in the sway of the trees and with the trickle of the stream. Feel the expansive energy of the sky, the mountains, river, or brook. Do this for ten minutes or perhaps longer. You will observe your body relaxing as it adjusts to peace. The longer you stay in this quiet energy, the quicker your body heals, returning to healthy functioning. You are returning your body and mind to its natural state. Your blood pressure drops, stress and tension release, digestion and sleep improve, the mind quiets.

Animals and babies don't work to be in relationship with God. They don't know anything but love until or unless they are taught otherwise. Babies, puppies, and kittens radiate love. They don't know any better. It's easy. They are naturally beautiful and magnetic. When you merge with love, you are too!

Discovering Stillness

Only in quiet waters things mirror themselves undistorted.
Only in a quiet mind is adequate perception of the world.
Hans Margolius

There is a cycle to life, a recognizable on-off rhythm. When we align with this rhythm, we experience a sense of rightness, perhaps centeredness. If we force action when it is not prescribed, we experience strain and struggle. We go against the grain. Life in resistance is constantly on the move: doing things and going places, pushing and forcing action. This may seem more comfortable because it is what we are used to, a habit. So, we end up going with the familiar and sidetracking ourselves because we have lost our natural rhythm.

To be at peace, we must adjust to a flow that is natural and healthy. You can feel this. Ask your body if you are in your natural rhythm. You will feel the answer to this question. To remain healthy, you must move in the current or flow of Spirit. It is the same thing.

Ambiguity often breeds a form of reactiveness. This discomfort drives us to search for ways to resolve the anxiety. Through discipline, this vagueness, or what I call *in-betweenness*, can be endured. It is a learned skill. Something is going to happen, but it hasn't happened yet. Ambiguity passes when it is time to act or take a new direction. As you remain centered in Spirit through practice, ambiguity dissolves and you will sense and honor the Universe's timing.

Many people avoid meditation because they think of it as work and difficult. They also fear that they won't do it perfectly. They really don't know how to quiet their minds. They have trained for a long time to have busy, chaotic minds. Therefore, meditation seems impossible.

Sometimes people fear what they will discover from meditation. Maybe they are not good enough or have broken some rule and are bad. They project their fear of unworthiness on to God and believe that they will be judged harshly. However, God is love and does not judge. The judger is themselves. Their lesson is to forgive and accept themselves as innocent children in the Universe, wandering around without a *play* book.

The way to quiet the fear-based mind is to train yourself to make love your center. Love, as the opposite of fear, houses no accusations or doubts. Love will guide you to release and rest from confusion. As you evolve, you will discover that fear is a contrived illusion and can be discarded.

What if you don't have to meditate perfectly? What if there is no such thing as perfect meditation? What if you find out that you are beautiful and loved? An innocent child of God? What if you don't have to do it at all? What if you can simply rest and let go, and God will do the rest? What if these are your true realities?

The Art of Giving

Do things for people,
not because of who they are or what they do in return,
but because of who you are.
Harold S Kushner

Giving is an under-used word in our society. Yet, the key to receiving or experiencing what you want is to give it first to others. The Bible says, *As you sow, shall you reap.* In physics, the law is *for every action there is an opposite and equal reaction.* Psychological circles state the principle as cause and effect. We have otherwise been taught that *what goes around comes around.*

All these statements say the same thing. If you want something, start the ball rolling in that direction by giving it away. Set up a specific cause to experience a specific effect. Experiment with this concept as though you were in a science lab. In truth, all life is an experiment. It is only through trying new things that we discover what works and what doesn't. Holding back, fear of not having enough, and obsessing over failure only keeps you stuck. It keeps you stuck. Find out what does work!

There are many people who complain about life. The car doesn't run right, their children are disrespectful, the boss is a tyrant, it rains too much, and prices are too high. Everything is wrong. No wonder that life is heavy and negative. These people are heavy and negative. Life reflects back to them whatever they put out in life. These people go to great lengths to see situations from a poor-me perspective. Their payoff is martyrdom, victimhood and, occasionally, sympathy. They claim this outcome through their words and actions. They live it and it cycles back from the world.

It is easy to find things to complain about. It takes more talent to search for the positives of a situation. Eventually, everyone must make a choice about what one wants to experience and what one is willing to do about it. If you blame and complain, your life will be miserable. Consequently, if you decide to live life as a positive possibility, be prepared to work at it and prosper because opportunity is everywhere.

Productive, joyous results come from well-intentioned causes. For example, a very simple truth is that, if you want to experience love, give it first. Reach out and care about those around you. Show interest, listen, see the good, and touch people in non-threatening ways. If you desire adventure, offer yourself new experiences, places, and people. If you want credit for your effort, compliment and give credit to others. Guaranteed, it will come back to you.

An extra bonus that automatically comes from having a giving heart is joy! When you see a child with a new toy or a friend who feels he is not alone because you are supporting him, or a family now has food, where before you had entered the picture, they did not, your heart will sing.

I knew a businessman who was informed about a family that not only had no money for Christmas gifts for their kids but was struggling to have food to eat. He decided to help them. He withdrew five $100 bills from his bank account and put the money in an envelope on which he wrote, *Merry Christmas*!

The next evening, he arrived at the family's house and put the envelope in an easy-to-see place on their front porch. He rang the doorbell and ran to hide behind some bushes.

A woman in a rag-tag sweater answered the door. Spotting the envelope, she picked it up and opened it. The man heard a deep *whush* as she took in a deep breath and let out a surprised yelp. "Thank you!" she called out to the night air.

The businessman was so *happy,* he walked on air for the next month. And so, we wonder, who was the giver and who was the receiver? It appeared that both were enriched by a simple act of kindness.

When we become too me-me oriented, we forget that self-centeredness, which focuses exclusively on self without consideration for others, brings a consequence of isolation, loneliness and unhappiness. It is okay to be attentive to personal goals and desires, but be sure to include others as you move along your way. After all, we are one big global family.

The golden rule is: *Give unto others as you would have them give unto you.* That is another way of saying, you reap the benefits of the intentions you sow (or focus on). So, what do you want? What are you willing to give?

Letting Go Opens the Door for New Opportunity

When everything has come and gone
what remains is the love that you are, residing in perfect stillness.
Author Unknown

When we feel we have what we want or we have reached the zenith of life, letting go is a challenge. But it is also an opportunity. Some consider letting go weak, like fragility, failure or loss. The fact is that letting go is freedom. It releases you to incredible new beginnings.

When Oprah Winfrey was told that she was too emotional to deliver the nightly news, there was a part of her that was relieved. It appeared that, even though her sensitivity made it difficult to be a news anchor, it was exactly the right quality to have a successful talk show. She released her news reporter-anchor job and found a new home as an interviewer-hostess on daytime talk television. Consequently, the *Oprah Show* was born. It dominated daytime television for twenty-five years, and she never looked back. One might say she not only did not resist but also, welcomed the change. You might also say that reporting the news enabled her to be a good interviewer and hostess. Therefore, letting go led to her next growth step. Just like it does for you.

Activity: What opportunities are present right now to give graciously just for the joy of it? What would you like to give? Care, love, kindness, money, resources? How might you proceed right now? Today?

The Freedom of Non-Attachment

Letting go means to come to the realization that
some people are a part of your history, but not a part of your destiny.
Steve Maraboli

Non-attachment is the ability to enjoy things, people, and circumstances without needing to control or possess them. Jack Schwarz, the founder of the Aletheia Foundation in Oregon, describes non-attachment as being fully involved but not affected by changes in situations or experiences. The most natural examples of non-attachment include the air that moves freely, water that flows casually to the river or ocean, waves that rise and fall gracefully and rhythmically launch themselves to the beach, the seasons that subside and spring forth, and the earth that moves freely on its axis. Each offers a sense of ease and flow that is not attainable with attachment.

Allowing life to flow freely allows you to receive maximum benefits from experiences and relationships. Experiences and relationships are born with a lifespan. The same is true with all nature. The flower or tree does not fight its natural progression. Only man fights the cycle of life.

Energy wants to flow freely through you, your life, situations and every moment. This energy shows itself as inspiration, imagination, creativity, ideas whose time has come, answers that show up as needed. It is all there all the time.

When you interfere with natural energy flow, you block abundance, joy, peace, and create body discomfort. When you refuse to give in to changes when the time has come, you inhibit your next phase of growth, and you invite chaos, turmoil and destruction.

Often, people hold on to the past and want things to stay the same, but that is not possible. Nothing in nature stays the same. The river you stepped into yesterday is a new river today. When it is time for a seed to blossom into a plant, it must. When it is time for a baby to be born, it will come. Free-flow is often seen as destruction because something must leave for something else to be born. The horse and buggy had to disappear as mechanized travel took over.

The requirement then, is to allow flow by not attaching to how things have been or how we require them to be. By not accepting change, we are perceiving with limited eyes and disavowing the possibilities that our actions have set up for the future.

When Orville and Wilbur Wright developed an airplane that could stay in the air for minutes, they opened the door to the space-age and people walking on the moon. When we see that all things lead to new possibilities, we are ready to move with the times.

It is as Jesus instructed when he said that we come into the greater kingdom (awareness) with the innocence of a child, ready for the adventure. We enter it with eyes and hearts open in willingness, allowing the day to fall into night and one season to melt into the next, attaching to nothing because we have everything.

Non-attachment, along with non-judgment and non-resistance, are three important aspects to enlightened living. When we live from our center, we are open to the next experience and phase of growth.

Recently, I spoke with a woman who was experiencing Parkinson's disease. She had a just sold her lovely home because she recognized it was time to move into a pristine assisted-living facility while she worked to heal her illness. But before she had acquiesced to let go of her house, her car had been stolen from the garage, her home had been ransacked, and the refrigerator had been left unplugged with $400 of food spoiled. These were the destructive incidences that pushed her into selling her house and moving on to a pastoral lifestyle in relative peace and harmony.

She recognized the time had come. She made her decision to transition to her next home because she felt the Universe was pointing her in that direction. She let go of struggle and moved on to ease, simplicity and beauty.

Judgments Reflect Attachment

The truth is, unless you let go,
unless you forgive yourself,
unless you forgive the situation,
unless you realize that the situation is over,
you cannot move forward.
Steve Maraboli

All judgments reflect attachment. All attachments result from irrational belief systems. An example: *It is of great importance to be liked and approved of by everyone.* Thus, when someone appears to *not like* you (approve), you could easily judge them and/or yourself. And the person who doesn't approve of you is definitely in judgement, because people who feel fine about themselves don't judge others. Being judged or judging others migrates to anger, resentment and criticism. Lots of wasted energy. It goes like this:

Irrational Belief = Attachment = Judgment and Criticism

The belief is that, to be considered a valuable person, everyone must like me. The attachment is to everyone liking you and to being judged valuable. Judgment and self-criticism result when it appears that someone has broken your self-inflicted rule and doesn't seem to like you. Result: *I've failed! I'm a failure! I was unable to live my irrational belief.*

There are many such irrational beliefs. When we live in an irrational state, believing we can control everything and everyone, we are in constant turmoil. We are not moving freely as air, water or ocean currents. We are going against nature and movement.

It is hard to achieve a non-attached state when we make our personal identity and value dependent on someone else's whim. The way to accomplish peace and joy is to let go. And not just let go, but release the situation by moving into harmony and joy, knowing that there is goodness on the other side of the change we are experiencing. That means we can enjoy the person and situation we are experiencing, but we must not hold on.

To accomplish *letting go* necessitates that your desire for something higher is greater than your desire to hold on. Ask yourself, *What is my strongest desire?*

It might get tricky here because *desire*, in itself, denotes attachment. So, the point would be to have the desire but not hang on to it. That means you take action to move in the direction of your choosing without clinging to the goal and negating the natural flow of life. What non-attachment offers is the possibility of something greater happening. With attachment to the way things have to be, we become myopic and can't see greater possibilities. We miss out!

It is important to pay attention, because the thing you want often comes to you in a completely different form and manner than you had expected. Often, it is way better. So, if you apply for a job and don't get it and another job presents itself, check it out. It might be the better opportunity.

I worked with a woman once who stated she wanted a personal relationship with a man. She wanted a boyfriend. The problem, as I saw it, was she was very prejudiced against men. In fact, she hated them. I told her that, since she hated man and was not ready to change her mind about that, the only man she would attract is a guy who hated himself. That idea did not particularly faze her. In her world, a boyfriend was a boyfriend.

A month or so later, she told me that there were two men who were interested in being her boyfriend. I asked her if they hated themselves. Her answer was *Yes*. They both had very low self-esteem. (If they didn't love themselves, they were unable to love anyone else.) Hence, her attachment to anger toward men kept her stuck in unloving relationships. Nothing was going to change on that front until she was willing to let go of her past wounds and allow a new insight or value to present itself. Point made! Attachment always reflects in limited (small) possibilities.

I love my home, the beauty, comfort, and peacefulness, but I am not attached to it. Consequently, if something happens that interferes with me living in my house, like a natural disaster, for instance, I can let go and move on to the next dwelling. I've done it many times.

There is nothing in life that cannot be replaced, and there is nothing in the material world that is permanent. Everything is in transition: relationships, possessions, situations, jobs, houses, all experiences. The only unchanging aspect is our connection with Spirit (God). It is unchanging and stable. The one thing that will never go away.

You may have a dear friend and, at some point, that friend may leave to experience a new adventure. You can love your time with that person while you have it, but if you hold on to it, decide it is to be forever, or that it is the end-all of friend-relationships, your attachment can turn love into anger, jealousy or resentment. When this happens, folks often look for someone or something to blame instead of realizing that everything in the mundane world is of short duration. Yet, the river is forever flowing and each day merges into the next.

Activity: To develop non-attachment and letting go, clean out your closet and release things that are no longer useable or relevant to your current style. Next, go to the basement or garage and pick a box to go through with the same intent: letting go and prioritizing. The easier it becomes to let go of mundane things that have lost their usefulness, the easier it will be to recognize intangibles that have worn out their effectiveness. That would be belief systems that are irrational and ineffective or possible *friendships* that have gone south over the years. You release attachment to that which has completed its service, making room for new people and things that match your consciousness now.

Look for a Higher Perspective

Nothing kills the ego like playfulness, like laughter.
When you start taking life as fun, the ego has to die.
It cannot exist anymore.
Osho

Choosing to *see* life from a higher perspective is an asset in discovering the power of non-attachment. Again, what is the purpose of this event, of this person appearing in my life? What is the opportunity? It may be that you have learned a new skill, or an event provided an answer, solved a problem, or aided in putting the puzzle pieces of your life together in a new way.

This is what higher vision is all about. You stop letting ego attachment determine your path and your reactions. You take a moment to move to your heart and listen to the guidance there. Spirit always guides you as you develop inner listening.

You may love your home, car, job, but don't become so attached that it destroys you if something were to happen to it. There are lots of places to call home, and lots of cars, friends, jobs and opportunities.

Let's say you have a business you wish to build. Pay attention. There are people who can help. There are skill-building classes, instructive books, and resources that move your goal closer. Even challenges offer the potential to strengthen commitment and create a more powerful stance to live your values.

These are examples of how life works as we develop the power of non-attachment and effortless ease. It does not mean we are not busy developing skills, seeking opportunities and managing challenges, but we do this with the knowing that the Universe has our back, that we are working in concert with Greater Intelligence and we trust this.

Exercise: Here is how to practice non-attachment. Create a clear mental picture of an experience you desire, write it down, and let go of *how* it is to come to fruition. To do that well, you must also let go of opinions, irrational beliefs, fear, obligations that don't enrich, and material objects that bog you down. Letting go frees the mind and the soul and *creates_space* for the natural intuitive flow of creativity to do its work. New concepts and actions, leading to the materialization of your desire, will present themselves when you are non-attached.

What you are doing is handing this desire to your higher mind. In time (sooner or later) this item will present itself in your life a way that you would never have imagined. That is the power of allowing God to be your silent and unfailing partner.

That is what higher vision is all about. You no longer let ego attachment dictate your actions and reactions. You take a moment to move to your heart and listen to the guidance there. Spirit always guides you and you get better at listening as you practice. As we move with the Universe, we develop trust and knowing that the Universe supports us and we are working in concert with It.

Non-Resistance Leads to Happiness

You don't have to control your thoughts.
You just have to stop letting them control you.
Dan Millman

Recognizing the natural flow of energy goes a long way to experiencing a life of peace, joy and fulfillment. Start by noticing the rhythm of nature, how effortlessly winter yields to spring and how nature bursts forth in an array of shades, shapes and textures. Then, summer temperatures turn warm and outdoor activities abound. Fall follows, gracefully erupting trees in glorious spectacles of color, and animals scurry to prepare for cold, stillness and retreat.

It is the same with man. There are cycles in life. You can recognize and accept them. Endings and beginnings. Death and rebirth. By choosing peaceful acceptance, you release the need to fight, resist, and struggle. Paying attention to your inner rhythm will intensify and embolden your efforts and lead to a life of flow and peace.

Here is a story that exemplifies this principle of non-resistance.

There was a little critter that lived in the water near the bank of a river. It fed off elements within the river. Sometimes there was food to eat and other times there wasn't. Either way, the critter spent its life clinging tightly to the bank because it was afraid. It believed that, if it let go of the bank, it would surely perish in the sweep of the treacherous river's current. Its fear escalated when the current was particularly strong. There were days when the critter was exhausted with the effort of clinging, yet it would not let go because it was consumed with terror of what might happen if it were swept away in the unknown flow of the river.

One day, overwhelmed with exhaustion, the critter could no longer hold on to the bank. It finally released its grip and surrendered to the river. Tumbled and tossed by the tide, it was swept downstream. In minutes, it landed in a beautiful pool of calm, pristine water. As the critter adjusted to the stillness of this newfound home, it looked around and saw that there was an abundance of food, obtainable within reach and without struggle. It dawned on the critter that, if it had trusted the river all along, it could have enjoyed this peaceful, lavish existence sooner.

Thus, it is with each of us. We can let go and trust the river/flow (Spirit), allowing it to take us where it will. Or we can hold on, fighting change, fearfully trying to control the status quo as we struggle. Letting go requires courage and faith. Holding on keeps you small, tense, and scared.

Of course, the river critter represents you and me. At various times, we have clung to the riverbank of our lives (the known) in fear of accepting the changes advancing upon us. We have clung in doubt and without trust, resisting the flow of life and where it will take us. Our greater good is in developing the strength, courage, and faith to let go and be taken to our next experience. It is to accept that something greater than our small egoic selves can devise a plan. By following its process, we can be led to an expanded experience that we may never have imagined. The truth is that life is always moving us toward expansion. As we flow with it, we live exalted lives. Releasing the old and moving on in gratitude is the way we grow into our full potential.

Situations change and, to live peaceful lives, you must adapt with them. Letting go is freedom. It releases you from the tired habits of the past and moves you to incredible beginnings that result in ease and expansion, just like the river critter.

What are you holding on to now? How can you begin to flow and grow with life?

The Expansive Power of Gratitude

By practicing gratitude, we change our entire magnetic field and attract opportunities for greater abundance and joy to our lives.

There is a wonderful legend about a wanderer in the desert who happened on a spring of clear, fresh water. He found the water delicious and his desire was to share this wonderful gift from nature. So, he excitedly filled his jug with this amazing nectar and proceeded to hurry off to share his treasure with his beloved king. The wanderer crossed a great distance, over many days, and eventually arrived at the palace to offer his gift to the king.

The king tasted the water and smiled. He then offered profuse gratitude to the wanderer for his kind gift.

The members of the court rushed forward to sample the water. They were expecting to taste cool, clean water. Instead, they found the water to be hot and stale. They gagged as they tasted it and spit it out.

A member of the court inquired of the king, "How could you give thanks for this spoiled water?"

The king smiled broadly as he divulged that it was not the water he had tasted, but the spirit in which it was given. The grateful king was focused on the loving intent of the wanderer.

Receiving a gift is an art unto itself. Remembering that, it is not the gift but the spirit of the giver that counts, can help us be better givers and receivers, plus cultivate an attitude of gratitude.

Gratitude, being an extension of love, keeps the mind centered on goodness. Since fear and love are opposites, when you focus on the goodness life offers, you are unable to be afraid. Instead, you reside in love. Gratitude may sound simplistic, but just as the members of the king's court did not comprehend the opportunity to feel thankful for the wanderer's gift, gratitude is often not practiced.

When most people gaze over their lives and perceive all they have achieved, both tangible and intangible, instead of feeling awed and appreciative, they frequently think, *Is that all?* Or, *But I don't have that thing, event, or relationship that I want.* Or, *What's next?* In other words, stopping to smell the roses is not part of the equation for them.

Do you consciously appreciate your friends, family, home, job, freedom, health, and income you've earned? It is easy to take these things for granted and think that what you have isn't enough.

My car isn't a BMW. It's an old Chevrolet.

I'm not president of the company. I'm only ______ [fill in the blank].

I don't make enough money, have enough prestige, live in the best part of town, or know the right people.

With this type thinking, attention is on what you don't have, on what's missing. It's on the negatives rather than the positives. This is called *fear-based* thinking. You never win or feel good about yourself when you focus on lack and live fearfully.

The old car transports you wherever you want to go. Many people don't even own a car. Your current job is a stepping-stone to wherever you go from there. The house you own represents the down payment on the next one. All your past learning experiences graduate you to the next level and prepare you for greater expression and service. You will more easily move to your next car, job, home, and elevated opportunities by graciously appreciating the ones you have already completed.

The law of gratitude dictates that, before you move on, you value your current job position and customers. As you do this, your expanded consciousness magnetizes new, greater opportunities and customers.

Gratitude is a law of nature. When we accept and are at peace with our circumstances, things begin to change naturally, easily. Deep, sincere gratitude sows the seeds that blossom in abundance. This is the magnetic principle of nature.

When people feel acknowledged and appreciated, they more readily acknowledge and appreciate you. When you are grateful for all you have experienced and achieved, even the *bad* stuff, your life and consciousness naturally expand. Your understanding that hardship and challenge build the characteristics of strength and leadership becomes apparent. You need these qualities to achieve whatever goal comes next.

There is a science to gratitude. As you explore the energy of gratitude, you discover the law of prosperity. When you genuinely feel grateful, your energy rises and expands. It aligns with your divinity. It connects you to God.

You can *feel* it. Think of something or someone for which you are grateful. Notice the feeling in your body as you do this. It feels light and expanded. Happy!

Now, consider someone or something for which you feel annoyed, angry, resentful or critical. You will notice your body shifting to a heavy, restricted state. Just like that, you have shifted energy.

Be sure to bring yourself back to gratitude. As you observe more, you will want to choose gratitude. You have the power of choice. Where are you placing your attention? It takes discipline to stay focused on gratitude. Just like a computer, the mind abides by your wishes.

For the most part, people do not recognize that they have this power of choice. Yet, as they develop mental discipline and make positive choices, they alter the trajectory of their lives. Manage your thoughts and the benefits will be astounding.

When you think thoughts of gratefulness, it is the same as thinking thoughts of having received. Gratitude for having already received your desire, immediately magnetizes the energy needed to manifest it in your space-time reality.

The quantum field of energy in which we live, breathe, and have our being, receives the impressions of your thoughts. The field is mutable, like Silly Putty. It automatically assumes the shape, intensity and quality of your thoughts. Thus, your thoughts become a template for this mutable energy to take form. Magnetic thoughts of gratitude expand energy and bring more of what you appreciate to you.

To say it another way, gratitude shifts universal energy. It manipulates it so that the ideas, hunches, connections and opportunities you need are drawn to you. That is how desires are made manifest.

Reverend Michael Beckwith says it this way: *You cannot have what you are not willing to be vibrationally.* (You must match your thoughts to your desires.)

Oprah Winfrey, the great television personality, demonstrates a good example of the workings of this law. She began life living with her grandmother, a maid in Mississippi in a house without indoor plumbing. Her grandmother wanted to train her to be a maid so she could work for a "*good* white" family. Oprah wasn't having it. She had her own dreams, bigger dreams.

Oprah was bright and excelled in school and had a natural ability to speak in public. For instance, she would recite the Sunday sermon to her classmates on Monday. She used her intelligence and innate skills for communication to move beyond her meager beginnings. She sought education and opportunity, and ended up creating a life of influence, wealth and success.

Throughout her development, Oprah kept a *Gratitude Journal.* At the end of each day, she recorded all the things for which she was grateful. She daily acknowledged the people she had met, what she had learned, and each event that had encouraged her growth. And now, she has made history as the first black female to become a billionaire. She is an icon and example to all, and she is not finished yet!

Universal law states that what you focus on increases. Oprah focused on gratitude and, through the law of increase, her position, opportunities, friendships, and wealth increased. She started working at a news desk and ended up owning her own cable television network. Her life is abundant. Yours can be, too.

This law of increase is indiscriminate and works for everyone. Start your day with appreciation for all the gifts and opportunities at hand. End your day with gratitude for all you have been given and received. Even be grateful for the seeming dark times. *Thank you for this incredible opportunity to grow and be more than I was before. Thank you for unleashing me and increasing me.*

One woman I know takes a trip to the grocery store whenever she begins to doubt the law of abundance. As she stands and gazes over the myriad types of fruits and vegetables, she is reminded of how truly great the Universe is. She sees abundance in the dozens of different breads, every kind of meat, aisles filled with condiments, a bakery full of sweets. Staggering abundance. Perhaps visiting a grocery store can remind you of abundance as well.

What a great world we live in. We have endless opportunities to express, experience, live freely, laugh, love, share and experience every kind of abundance. If something doesn't seem to work, make another choice and arrive at your goal a different way. There are a myriad routes to the same destination.

As you make gratitude your everyday experience, you will attract greater potentials. You will develop determination to climb over obstacles and blast through walls. You will become unstoppable and your energy will expand and soar. The dynamic power of gratitude opens you to the field of possibilities.

Elizabeth Gilbert, Author of *Eat, Pray, Love,* suggests, *You need to learn how to select your thoughts just the same way you select your clothes every day. This is a power you can cultivate. If you want to control things in your life so bad, work on the mind. That's the only thing you should be trying to control.*

Activity:

Start a gratitude journal and record your blessings every morning and evening, or at least every night before you go to bed. At night, while you sleep, your mind will build on your gratitude list to create the events for the next day.

Begin each day with statements of gratitude.

I am grateful for this magnificent day and my continuous blessings.

I am grateful for sunshine and a great meeting with my boss.

I am grateful for nutritious food and fun friends.

Thank you for the beautiful trees, grass, and flowers.

Keep going. Make the list new every day.

Notice the changes that occur in your life. Observe the blessings that show up. Perhaps someone buys your meal or brings you coffee. You may receive a great coupon for your favorite store. Someone invites you to a party. The birds are singing joyfully. The sunset is gorgeous.

Kindness Ignites the Soul

Love and kindness are never wasted. They always make a difference. They bless the one who receives them, and they bless you, the giver.
Barbara De Angelis

One thing you will notice about spiritually evolved people is that they are kind and compassionate. Nicht That Hahn, a well-known author and wise Buddhist monk, is a great example. Hahn has been teaching spiritual principles for a long time. In his book, *Peace*, he tells a story of a group of Vietnamese refugees who arrived at his refugee center in France. They had experienced a difficult journey on the boat that carried them through treacherous waters from Vietnam to France. During their perilous flight, pirates captured their boat. Because of vastly limited resources in Vietnam, many survived by becoming pirates. So it was that, dealing with pirates, was a common threat for refugees traveling by boat.

The pirates seized the boat, terrorizing the passengers. They also grabbed and raped a twelve-year-old girl. When the encounter was over, the distraught girl jumped into the ocean and drowned. As the refugees described the incident to the monk, he clearly saw that they were traumatized by the event.

Nicht That Hahn noted that it was very easy to empathize with the Vietnamese boat people and the young girl who had been raped and drowned, yet, he observed, no one seemed to have compassion for the pirates. His point was that, if one considered the circumstances of the pirates, it might radically alter their understanding of what it takes for a person to perform the heinous act of rape. What suffering had the pirates experienced to have hardened to such a degree? Hahn's thought carried forth that many babies were born along the rivers in Vietnam and often, because of extreme poverty, were given little care or abandoned altogether. Frequently, these children were the ones that turned toward piracy. They did not receive love, care or nurturing. For the most part, they were abandoned very young and left to their own devices. Thus, the pirates' lives reflected grabbing what they could and stealing what they needed. It was the way they had learned to survive.

Even in such dire circumstances, Hahn considered that we must be willing to rise above events to view the whole picture. The pirates were also victims. To condemn without empathy only exacerbates the situation. What good did judgment provide? Could we see a bigger problem that needed remedying? Did we achieve a clearer understanding through judging, blaming, and criticizing? Perhaps compassion toward the perpetrators and what they had gone through to become pirates might eventually bring healing, peace and solutions for a better world.

Furthermore, Hahn stated that we all have these qualities within us. We are the victimized girl. We are her family, the boat people, and the pirates. We have all of these aspects within us. Condemning does not offer remedies. Compassion does.

Nicht That Hahn suggests that compassion for all concerned helps us move beyond upsetting circumstances to register a larger issue. With empathy, we recognize the trauma and fear all have experienced. This leads to unconditional, spiritual love that has the capacity to heal. By releasing attachment to being *right* and judging others *wrong*, we learn how to love. This form of release lifts awareness and allows the energy and magic of the Universe to work through each person.

Small Acts of Kindness

Kindness can become its own motive.
We are made kind by being kind.
Eric Hoffer

Mother Teresa stated: "Kind words can be short and easy to speak, but their echoes are truly endless." If you have any doubt about the effectiveness a small act of kindness can have in lifting someone's day or mood, take heed of this comment by former American football quarterback, Kurt Warner. "Sometimes you don't want to realize it, or you think that an autograph isn't going to do that much, or to stop and say 'Hi' doesn't really do that much. But through the course of time, I've realized the impact I can have in whatever way, whatever facet. People are watching, and people do pick up on those things." You might think that small acts make a difference when it is football's great Kurt Warner performing them, but that is only one side of the story.

There are other stories of kindness that have made huge impacts in people's lives. Three-and-a-half-year-old Erika gave all of her Halloween candy to another little girl who was wheelchair-bound and unable to go door to door. Two friends spent a lot of time and energy to carefully remove an injured cat from certain death on a highway. A generous mother, annually and anonymously, donated food, clothing, toys and games to a poor family.

Finally, there was an elderly woman ordering food at a Chinese restaurant when she noticed a homeless man rummaging through his pockets to assemble change to pay for the eggroll he had ordered. The woman, who didn't have much herself, bought an additional cup of soup and quietly had it delivered to the homeless man as an addition to his eggroll.

Think about it. Who do you know who could use a compliment, a love note, a message of appreciation or praise, a thoughtful act, someone to ease their life in some small way? Can you find it within yourself to sing someone's praises or offer a flower, a smile, or pat on the back?

There are numerous things the world could benefit from having more of, and none is more important than kindness. When you choose to be kind, you not only assist others, but you help yourself as well. There is scientific evidence that being kind makes you and those around you happy.

Dr. Sonja Lyubomirsky, a psychology professor at the University of California, Riverside, did a study wherein students were assigned to do five random acts of kindness per week for six weeks. At the end of the study period, it was noted that the students' levels of happiness had increased by 41.66%. It was concluded that, being kind, had a profoundly positive effect on happiness.

There is an old dictate: *It is better to give than receive*. Perhaps this statement is not referring so much to you having to be a giving person, but to the positive psychological results that come from giving. However, it need be said that the motive behind giving is what provides its meaning. In other words, do you give out of your fullness or your lack? Do you give because you should? Or because you find pleasure in it?

Fighter pilot Jim Stockdale, who was held as a Vietnam prisoner of war for eight years, states that, "You are your brother's keeper. Period. The question is not what's in it for me? The question is, how can I help?"

What's in it for me is an oft repeated statement in our world. Frequently, children are raised with the notion that having an abundant life is getting the best education and making as much money as possible. They are taught that, to live the good life, their attention should be on bigger and better material stuff. Kindness, as a building block to character, is not necessarily included in the scenario. But luckily, there are those who teach that, with greatness comes the question, "How can I help?"

Do you remember the story of the Good Samaritan? Martin Luther King, Jr. taught that the first question the priest and the Levite asked was, *If I stop to help this man, what will happen to me?* But the Good Samaritan reversed the question. *If I do not stop to help this man, what will happen to him?*

In ancient Greek, the word *hero* is rooted in love and compassion. Plutarch taught that the heroic ideal is to care. True heroism isn't about strength, boldness, or courage, but compassion. The Greek idea of a hero was a protector. This is not to say that heroes are perfect, for most Greek heroes teetered between inner conflict, self-doubt, and altruism. Yet, the great ones tipped toward the power of empathy and compassion. They believed that empathy was a source of strength, not weakness. The more you see yourself in others and connect with their distress, the more inner endurance, wisdom, cunning, and determination you tap into. Heroes extend beyond duty to protect and to love.

Franklin D. Roosevelt went along with this notion when he said, "Human kindness has never weakened the stamina or softened the fiber of a free people. A nation does not have to be cruel to be tough."

So, again, think about it. Who do you know who could use a compliment, a love note, a message of appreciation or praise, a thoughtful act, someone to ease their life in some small way? And can you find it within yourself to sing someone's praises or offer a flower or a smile or pat on the back?

If you want the world to be a better place, it has to start with you. Are you ready? What are you willing to do?

Activity:

Consider a situation that has evoked strong negative feelings. Examine each person involved in the experience and ask yourself. What was each individual feeling? Where or in what way was he/she wounded? Close your eyes and imagine this. As you realize the fact that wounded people wound others, feel compassion for the pain that each one has suffered or experienced. This is not about endorsing harmful behavior. Just look behind it and awaken to its cause.

Notice when you are feeling impatient, resentment or mean-spirited. Stop and take note of how these feelings started. Did you feel shunned? Are you exhausted? Have you given yourself validation and love? Have you taken a break or a vacation? With a little self-examination, you will discover personal needs that have gone unnoticed. When you do, take action to remedy these needs. That means be kind to yourself, too!

To feel better, do something kind for someone else. It can be the simplest thing: a smile, compliment, holding the door, provide a resource, send a thank you note. The list is endless. The rewards of feeling happy are boundless.

Forgive Yourself and Everyone Else

The weak can never forgive. Forgiveness is the attribute of the strong.
Mahatma Gandhi

Once there was a free bird. She floated on the wind drafts and caught midges for lunch. She flittered as the summer rain trickled and was like many other birds. But she had a habit. Every time some event occurred in her life, whether good or bad, the bird picked up a stone from the ground to remember it. Daily, she sorted through her stones, laughing over joyful events and crying as she remembered sad ones. Wherever she went, the bird took the stones with her. This included flying in the sky or walking on earth. She never forgot about them. Over the years, the bird collected a lot of stones. She still sorted them, remembering all the stories of the past. With the weight of these past events carried in the stones, flying became more difficult. One day, flying was impossible.

The bird that was free a while back could no longer walk on earth or fly in the sky. She was unable to move at all on her own. She could not catch midges, and only the occasional rain gave her moisture. Nevertheless, the bird bravely endured these hardships as she guarded her precious memories. After a while, the bird died of starvation and thirst. All that was left was a pitiful bunch of worthless stones.

Does this bird remind you of anyone? Perhaps yourself? Often, we carry the burden of past memories. occupying the creative space of the mind, and we are no longer able to live in the present time and respond to the gifts of the moment.

Carrying the past is *heavy.* It inhibits forward movement because the past is not the present and the present is the gift of *this* moment. This story is about letting go of the past. Forgiveness is the technique we use to do that. In fact, the key to living a peaceful life is forgiveness.

Some people confuse forgiveness with condoning bad behavior, but that is not what forgiveness is about. You can let go of a grievance without condoning negative behavior. People have their own reasons for being ruthless, greedy, angry and resentful. None of this has anything to do with you. We all operate from our developed state of consciousness with our own memories and values. This is what makes spiritual progress an individual matter.

Because of the ornery nature of the ego, an undisciplined person can feel uncomfortable and even mean-spirited toward those who are different. Exalted masters train their followers to be non-reactive (not shocked or intimidated) toward materially-minded folks who do not understand the path of the spiritual devotee.

Jesus instructed his followers that: *When you are reviled or made fun of because you walk a different walk, you are to take no heed, for you are blessed in Heaven.* It was clear to him that there are many people who are not ready to separate themselves from their material or egoic desires to experience the higher energy of spiritual love. He told them: *When you enter a town and you are not received, shake the dust from your feet and move on.*

This is to say that there are many who do not understand or appreciate spiritual practices and can be intimidated by those who actively pursue growth. But that must be of no consequence to the seeker after these things.

The story of the Gerasene Demonic (in the Bible) illustrates this dynamic of turning away from that which would heal. As the story goes, Jesus and his disciples docked their boat in the territory of Gerasene and, forthwith, Jesus healed a demonic man who had been chained in the cemetery. This man's mind was chained to the past (symbolized by cemetery) and that was insanity. The man had many demons, which reflected his divergent painful memories and numerous emotional wounds. After Jesus healed the man by casting out his insane thoughts (anger, resentment, guilt, shame, and grief), the man, against the instructions of Jesus, went into the town and informed the people of his incredible recovery. What followed was the town people going to Jesus and asking him to leave their territory. Apparently, these folks preferred to live in the past and found the transformation of the demonic too much to manage.

This story is a perfect depiction of the demented mental state of man wanting to remain in his disillusioned state, rather than permit the light of peace and love to enter, cleanse and bring healing.

No matter what comes at you in this world; you maintain your stance in goodness, peace, mercy, compassion and love. By so doing, you are blessed in spirit. You are elevated beyond the illusion of ego and right and wrong to the greater reward of spiritual oneness with love.

The Kingdom of heaven (peace) can only be reached with an open heart. Those who would cause harm to you or anyone are wounded beings. They are projecting their own pain on to others. Their minds have been twisted by misunderstanding and egoic interpretations and blame.

If they are present in your world, they are part of your healing and you of theirs. You bring healing to both by forgiving them, for they know not what they do. They are living in their wound and projecting their painful reality to external events and people. They are afraid and have closed themselves to the possibility of nurturing and kindness. Their walls of distrust have grown thick. You, as a vessel of love, must see beyond their pain and refuse to participate in it.

As you make this decision, you have pulled away from the drama of victimhood. It is not relevant to you. As you disengage from negative ideals, the illusion of hatred and fear dissolves and you are free. In your attainment of freedom, you have opened a doorway to peace for you and the other, if the other would have it.

In other words, within the mental framework of forgiveness, you embrace the Light within which is the truth of your being. You recognize that, no matter the peril or challenge, your dedication is to live in peace, not letting the low energy of anger or hate have entrance to your mental space. In that way, you are aligned with the peace that passes understanding, the peace of God. In other words, you have elevated your energy to align with God.

No matter what promise the temptation of revenge holds, it will always give in to sorrow in the end. You cannot experience peace while you hold grudges or attack-thoughts or guilt over what you did or did not do. All are released as you hand these dark thoughts to Spirit. That is the meaning of the story of the Gerasene Demonic.

An incredible truth is that people think they can get through life without making mistakes and yet, the whole experience of life is trial and error. No one has been handed a manual on how to get through life without getting bruised. So, why is it we are so hard on ourselves when we misstep? Earth life is a mistake-making proposition.

Earth school is where we learn, grow and figure things out. If we already knew this stuff, we wouldn't even be hanging out here. The key to being happy is to accept our slip-ups and blunders as part of the journey and keep motoring on. Just as you don't criticize a baby for getting up and falling down as he learns to walk, you don't down yourself for the same thing. We are all learning how to walk.

Do you remember the story of the Prodigal Son? The son left his wealthy father's house and went out into the world, blew his inheritance on gambling and various questionable activities, hung with an unsavory crowd, and ended up eating garbage from the pig's trough. We might say that he, basically, screwed up. Yet, it was after he had hit bottom that he woke up to the fact that he could return home to a loving father, a beautiful home. Even if he were to live out his days as a servant in his father's house, it would be a good life. That is when the magic happened because, as he started his journey home, his father came to welcome him and told him he held no animosity or grievance. In fact, it was the father's great pleasure to give him his kingdom.

Wow! The bottom line is that it doesn't matter how many mistakes you make. There is always opportunity and redemption waiting for you. Forgive yourself because you are the one holding your feet to the fire. Let go of all the things you believe you did wrong. You are just clunking around, trying to get it straight. Then, forgive everyone else because they are doing the same thing.

It is true that people really are doing the best they know how to do. Hopefully, as we continue to practice, we learn more and we get better. That is what forgiveness is all about. We are doing what we have been trained to do and, as we fall, we learn to pick ourselves up and try again. Forgive yourself and everyone else.

Graduating to a New Reality

> *With everything that has happened to you, you can either feel sorry for yourself or treat what has happened as a gift. Everything is either an opportunity to grow or an obstacle to keep you from growing. You get to choose.*
>
> Wayne Dyer

Do you remember when you were in kindergarten and you sat in a little chair behind a tiny desk. Well, guess what? You now possess a beautiful adult body that no longer fits in that teeny desk or scenario. In the same way, trying to operate from old, outmoded thought patterns that continually bring anguish, no longer work either. In the same way, memories that bring pain need to go. They create anxiety and do not serve you. Self-beratement is the same. It doesn't help!

Just because you belong to a family, social group or tribe does not mean you have to allow the expectations and demands of others to be a source of unhappiness and stress. This is especially true if you want to express authentically and be at peace.

Other people are not the source of your discomfort. You are! You can label people as annoying, troublesome or despicable. These are your projections. As you look at people differently, as wounded or lost, you will find forgiveness easy. Most of us have been handed a very inefficient playbook and we have been trying to make it work. A lot of it goes like this: *These are the good people and these are the bad people.* It doesn't work and it is an outright lie.

Often, we busy ourselves deciding how others should be, and when they are not that— respectful, considerate, kind or thoughtful, we get angry. They are not following the rules: your rules! Projecting your rules on to others and interpreting them through your standards is anxiety-provoking.

We really don't know what others have gone through to become the people they are, so categorizing them in good and bad columns is simplistic and irrational. It creates problems, particularly for you. Step back and look at each person objectively. For instance, Aunt Hannah has a knack for finding something wrong with everything and everybody. It is her quirk. It is not your job to change her. You can be disgruntled by her forbearance at finding fault, or you can find humor in it. You can become unnerved by Aunt Hannah's criticalness, or just observe it as her quirk. It is a projection of her own unhappiness, the way she finds fault with herself.

You can even make a mental caricature of Aunt Hannah and remind yourself that she plays her cartoon-self quite well. This gives you a chance to detach from your need to take her seriously and reframe your reaction. You would never get mad at the Road Runner or Bugs Bunny for their misdeeds. You actually find their redundancy humorous. Okay, same deal with Aunt Hannah. When you can step back and detach with a chuckle from Aunt Hannah's behavior, you will also be able to do the same with your own. Yes, on occasion you are also Aunt Hannah.

The key to happiness is taking care of your own business and letting others take care of theirs. In time, you might find these strange behaviors humorous or even quaint. The unalterable and ever-effective way to experience peace is forgiveness. Everyone is simply doing what they have been taught to do and what, in their minds, seems appropriate. They are also bearing the consequence of their actions. Perhaps they have never questioned their tactics. Criticizing has not made Aunt Hannah a happy person.

A wise, grounded person steps away from others' judgments and expectations and chooses, instead, to shower these same folks with compassion and forgiveness. As a result, one is doing what masters have suggested for eons. *Forgive them for they know not what they do.* In other words, they don't understand that they hurt themselves more than they hurt anyone else. Perhaps their wounds do not allow introspection.

Rather than keeping yourself wound up, be radical and decide to be grateful for others' presence in your life as it offers an opportunity to see yourself more clearly. It is like the Buddhist monk who, when informed that he would be dealing with a very difficult teacher, said, "Oh, good. I can practice!" Oh, good, we can all practice!

It is true, life is nothing if not practice. Each time you let go of struggle and anxiety, you grow a bit stronger and wiser. So, yes, practice. The truth is that nothing anyone does has anything to do with you. Each person is expressing his own level of development. The quicker you come to terms with that truth, the faster you will grow and transform. In the process, the caterpillar, *you*, becomes the butterfly. And you are free!

Forgiveness Stories and Technique

The world is full of magic things,
patiently waiting for our senses to grow sharper.
W.B. Yeats

During the Rwanda genocide in Nigeria during the mid-nineties, Immaculee Ilibagiza's entire family was brutally murdered. During the horrible event, she managed to escape, along with seven other women, by hiding in a small bathroom. For nine months, while confined in this small bathroom, she listened to people being brutally murdered just yards away. It was traumatizing and humbling.

Yet, Ilibagiza chose to forgive the people who were caught up in the blaze of murder of thousands of her countrymen and behind the death of her family. She knew that holding bitterness and anger would eventually destroy her. She wanted to bring something positive out of her horrendous experience. As a result, she wrote a best-selling book called, *Left to Tell,* and established a charitable fund to help orphaned children who survived the genocide.

Ilibagiza's story emphasizes our soul desire for peace. Let it be your intention, as it was hers, that no matter how rocky the path you walk, with undaunted patience and resolute determination, you will achieve it. By merging your consciousness to love and looking to discover deeper meanings, you attain the Kingdom of Heaven.

The act of forgiving has multi-purposes. When you forgive an attack, you are releasing a mental image that has kept you hostage. You are opening space in your mind for new life to enter. When you hold on to negative feelings and associations, you are directing your life toward more of the same, which proves an unpleasant future. Besides retaining a victim consciousness, you are using an upsetting event as a template for more of the same to enter your life. It is like handing your life to the devil, if there were such a thing. You cannot experience beauty in the present moment when you hold on to negative imagery of the past.

Another story that illustrates forgiveness occurred in a small logging town in Oregon. During World War II, a Japanese soldier named Nobus Fujita set about bombing the coastal forest range in Oregon. Later, after the war, Fujita felt remorse for his actions. He returned to Brooking, the small town where he had bombed the surrounding forests, to ask for forgiveness. To illustrate his regret and plea for forgiveness, he presented the town with a 400-year-old samurai sword that had been handed down in his family for generations. The town received the sword and forgave him. They hung the sword in the public library and pronounced Fujita an Ambassador of Good Will. Fujita could move on and the town felt resolved of the matter.

Forgiveness is about cleaning your mental state so that the energy of love can enter. If you are obsessed with past grievances, there is no space for love or peace. It is the same as taking poison and expecting someone else to die. Anger, resentment, shame, guilt and hateful thoughts are toxic. If they are your thoughts, you are the one that suffers. It doesn't matter what person you direct them toward. You still get the repercussions.

Consider your mind a blank screen and that you are placing on that screen the things that have meaning for you, the things you choose to give energy. If the scene you create is pastoral, you feel peaceful. If what dominates your thoughts is negative, your mind is frustrated and chaotic. If you put vengeance and anger on the screen, you will find your life dark and unfriendly. As Ilibagiza realized, these emotions would eventually destroy her. They will destroy you, too.

The desire or longing for peace has to outweigh any momentary pleasure in revenge. To establish the mind in peace and grace, one must set aside humanity's need to win or be right and look to a greater reward of spiritual connection. Persistence in taking the high road of love leads to bliss.

Purity of the heart gives one contact with God. *The yogi* (person) *who has completely calmed the mind and controlled the passions and freed them from all impurities* (anger thoughts) *and who is one with Spirit – verily, he has attained supreme blessedness.* Bhagavad Gita

Forgiveness technique: Here is a process to achieve a peaceful mind when it appears there has been a grievous act against you, or even if you have held a grievous thought against someone else. This technique is age-old, dating back to ancient cultures, including the original Hawaiians.

Start by envisioning the person with whom you wish to make peace in your mind. Speak to him from the level of spiritual love saying: "I love you. I'm sorry. Please forgive me. Thank you."

Continue this process until you feel peace. As you release each egoic need to be angry, peace will flood your awareness and you will be able to release the person and incident as though it never happened. For in your world, it didn't happen, because you have wiped the energy of disharmony from your inner screen, you mind.

In this process, you are asking for forgiveness from Spirit because you have chosen (on some level) to participate in the drama that has trapped your soul. You are thanking Spirit for the opportunity to be cleansed of the disruptive energy that your ego (personality) has held on to while engaged in the drama

Peace as a Priority

There is no other spiritual teacher than your own soul.
Swami Vivekananda

Stress is created in the mind. Situations do not create stress. Your beliefs about them do. Jim sees a yard full of leaves and starts pressuring himself to rake it. Meanwhile, his next-door neighbor, Harry, observes the same situation. Recognizing he has other priorities, he walks right past the yard without guilt or consternation. Jim can't release the obsession to clean up the mess. Harry has no pressure, because he has placed his peace of mind above the yard waste.

Jim carries a belief that, in order to be a good person, you must have a well-maintained yard. Even though he knows there is no time for yardwork, he is burdened. Instead, he could choose to focus on higher priority matters. This would necessitate self-control and a redefinition of the prerequisites to being a *good person*.

Irrational beliefs of this sort, and the ensuing pressure they create, keep the mind disorganized and troubled. Contrarily, peace can be achieved by making it the priority. Let yourself off the hook for now. You'll get to the yardwork later. What's more important than peace of mind?

Putting a peaceful mindset at the top of your list makes sense. Many are unwilling to put themselves on their list at all, much less at the top. *I'll get to my needs when everything else is finished.* It's no surprise then, when the day is over, you're still waiting your turn.

If we each dedicated an hour daily to practicing a peaceful mindset, the world would be calmer, brighter, and more hopeful. It could be as easy as leisurely walking, appreciating the sunshine, glorifying in nature, sitting quietly, fantasizing a perfect life, reading a good book, smelling the flowers, breathing deeply, writing yourself a love note, laughing, listening to calming music, meditation. The possibilities are endless.

Often, this kind of restructuring happens when illness strikes in a family. Suddenly, the messy yard, dusty furniture, or other important work loses significance. Health comes first. There is no guilt as tasks are ignored. The patient comes first. Perhaps you are the patient. The thing is, you don't have to wait for an emergency to include yourself on the priority list. Does anger, people pleasing and worry about the neighbors come before generating calmness? What beliefs do you hold that interfere with serenity? Maybe it is time to reorder the list.

Humility

When someone asked the Dalai Lama
what he wanted to be remembered for, he replied,
"It is okay if I am not remembered."

Many consider the idea of humility as deeming themselves less than or bowing down to others. In a way, they are right and, in another way, they are also wrong. True humility is stated by Jesus as *Of myself I do nothing. It is the Father within who doeth the work.* In this statement, Jesus gave credit for his work to the Spirit of God that flowed through him.

This same Spirit also flows through you. You have free will to do with it as you wish. In fact, all creativity is born as a result of this flow. Your level of evolution demonstrates your intent in using this energy and flow. You might say that beauty testifies to its master.

You are a vehicle and Spirit is the energy that animates you as it flows through you as energy and inspiration. You, of yourself can do nothing without this energy and inspiration. It is the energy that runs your body, causing your lungs to inspire and expire, your blood to pump, your skin and organs to regenerate, and your muscles to move. It is the Spirit that ignites your brain with thoughts and inspiration. You choose how you want to use these.

When you focus in a direction, like a problem to be solved, for instance, Spirit provides the resolution. If you focus the mind on wellness, it provides that. If you center your intention on illness, the energy follows your design and flows to dis-ease. Spirit is unconditional and flows where you direct it.

When we live in survival mode, we survive. When we lift our energy and imagination with the motive of love (highest frequency), beauty comes forth, whether it is in the action of nurturing a child, planting a garden, cooking a meal, cleaning a house, taking out the garbage out or whatever. It is all accomplished in unity with divinity. All works are sacred when addressed with humility.

Mohandas Gandhi was the epitome of humility as he led India to freedom from Britain. In his writings, he made his intention clear. Everything he did in life was to bring him closer to God. The types of food he ate, the clothes he wore, his actions, all were in alignment with his developing connection with Spirit. He lived from this highest, most dynamic intelligence. He was the change that he wanted to bring to the world. It energized him as he led India to freedom. And the people followed him because they saw the purity of his heart in action.

The same is true of all truly great leaders who work to raise their followers to new heights of insight, imagination and understanding. Paramahansa Yogananda came to America to bring enlightenment through yoga (union). He didn't have to give up his life in India to do it, but he did do it because that was his inner directive. He was a servant of the divine flow of energy that poured through him. When he spoke to packed auditoriums, he did not follow a scripted presentation. He let Spirit speak through his heart. People felt it and wanted more. His work brought new light to the western world.

Perhaps Spirit has whispered in your ear a role you are to play or an action to take. Perhaps you do not understand the plan that is unfolding, but you know it is right because you feel it. As you open to these high whisperings, they get louder and, soon, you develop partnership with the divine. As you do this, you also will say, *Of my own self, I do nothing. It is the Spirit that flows through me that does the work.* And with knowing that, you will find your work radiating with light and life because you have made yourself a servant of the divine.

Chapter 8: Freedom - Breaking Through

The Turning Point

Accept – then act.
Whatever the present moment contains, accept it as if you had chosen it.
This will miraculously transform your whole life.
Eckhart Tolle

Often times, a seemingly insignificant event becomes a catalyst, causing people to make radical changes in their lives. This happened near the end of the nineteenth century when a wealthy boy got into a fistfight with an impoverished boy. Ultimately, the rich youngster won the skirmish. As the poor boy rose from the dirt, he asserted that, if he had the same nourishing food to eat as his opponent, he would have won the match.

Hearing this pronouncement stunned and horrified the affluent youth. For it had never occurred to him that others might not have such basic necessities as healthy food. That moment served as a turning point in the rich boy's life. Because of this startling new information, he chose to give up all appearances of wealth and to dedicate his life to serving humanity with particular focus on helping poor and needy people. Thus, Albert Schweitzer became a physician, missionary, musician, philosopher and philanthropist. His work took him all over the world and culminated in him receiving the Nobel Peace Prize in 1952.

Schweitzer recognized early in life that wealth provided him advantages and opportunities that others did not enjoy. This profound realization inspired him to use his gifts to assist others. He felt that service to humanity was the key to lasting happiness. He commented, "I don't know what your destiny will be, but one thing I know: The only ones among you who will be truly happy are those who have sought and found how to serve."

Everyone has gifts that can be put to use, either in focusing solely on their own success and/or helping others. Every time you reach your hand out to others to assist them to be better, the whole, as a whole, is benefited.

Mother Theresa put it this way: "Be kind and merciful. Let no one ever come to you without coming away better and happier." Albert Schweitzer made that his goal. Perhaps we could do the same.

From Breakdown to Breakthrough

If you've made mistakes in the past
but have now learned not to repeat them,
you *brighten the world like a moon when released from a cloud.*
Thanissaro Bhikkhu, *Why Shame Gets a Bad Rap*

Often, what some consider a breakdown is really a breakthrough. What would happen if we recognized that breaking through our small-minded reality might require breaking down? I have seen it many times. A person asks for a new situation, a new way, a new beginning, and something crazy happens like an illness, accident, getting fired from a job, or a natural disaster. Suddenly, the old life is swept away, just like that, In the time span of days, weeks or months, a new beginning is birthed. Most of the time people call it tragic. I am not sure about that, because it seems that starting a new life requires sweeping the old one away on a tidal wave of change.

Many times, I have congratulated someone for having gone

through what they depict as hell, meaning they survived a struggle or trauma. Often, they are so fixated on judging the event traumatic that they don't realize they have just been profoundly transformed (blessed). Who they were is no longer who they are. So, in a way, they missed the magic of the moment.

It is a basic premise that people want to judge events, and it is in categorizing things as good or bad that they lose the ability to see things as they are.

To say it differently, if you are heart-set on a new experience, like travel, career, relocation, relationship, fame, whatever, and, at the same time, are stuck in the way things are or should be, unwilling to rearrange your life or take a risk, it might be that the Universe sticks its hand in and blows up your life. It could also mean that, when chaos has entered and things seem untenable and out of control, what is really happening is a breakthrough to a new chapter, phase or deeper dimension of experience. What if the only way to encounter a miracle or deeper state of consciousness is by letting go of everything known and starting over? Perhaps a shakeup is the only way the Presence of God can enter your heart.

Breakdowns and breakthroughs are necessary because the ego or small mind holds on with steel fists attempting to control life. It has its own idea of how things should be and white knuckles for security, even when there is no such thing. It pretends to know the way, the answer and methodology and is completely lost in its knowing. It is like a child pretending to be an adult when it has no experience.

The ego has rules to live by that are generated by a narrow view. It has its idea of what is perfect, based on the narrow experiences of the past, not possibilities for the future. Therefore, breakdowns, when everything seems out of control and overwhelming, are necessary so that the linear mind can recognize its own limitations. It is through the cracks of our perceived ideas that light can shine through to a new reality. That is what we are to do: crack open a small linear perspective to let the Light of the greater mind shine through and introduce a new way of being.

Jack was a high-level executive in a manufacturing company, the head engineer. Some mishap occurred. The finger got pointed at Jack. The incident ended his tenure of twenty-five years at the company, from which he had figured he would retire. At first, he was mad and resentful. Then, he woke up and said to himself, *I have always wanted to start my own business and never would have done it as long as I was working at the company.*

That was when Jack started living because that was when he used his imagination to create a successful technology business. It was also when he began scheduling time for travel and fun, when he began living a new, expanded experience. Life took Jack and shook him all around and set him down in a new reality that ultimately fulfilled his deepest desires.

What about you? Do you need a breakdown to have a breakthrough?

Expand Your Possibilities

You have to grow from the inside out.
None can teach you.
None can make you spiritual.
There is no other teacher but your own soul.
Swami Vivekananda

Albert Einstein's unified field theory states that the Universe is made up of energy. Everything is energy: your body, furniture, books, car, house, ideas, thoughts. Everything is part of the Universe or the Unified Field. All energy equivocates to possibilities. We live in a magnificent field of possibilities. Yes, anything is possible until we create blocks and become resistant. This means we can do or be anything until we hold ourselves in a status quo or negative pattern and refuse to change.

People become glued or hypnotized into a set of possibilities that keeps them in stasis. They repeat the same thing year after year. Same thought process, same behaviors, same outcomes. They say this is how it is. This is who I AM. It is their mental hypnosis. Creating just one crack in that veil can open the mind to vast potential. *Why do I have to do it this way? Why do I have to believe this or accept that?* This questioning begins the crack.

To stay in a repetitive pattern that does not produce joy, excitement, abundance, love and clarity is disavowing the field of possibilities. Do something different. If you always vacation in the mountains, go to the beach instead. Or be bold and leave the country altogether. If you always eat hamburgers and pizza, order squid or Thai food. Jump out of the mold. Shake up your consciousness. Explore your adventurous Self. It is there. Wake up. There is more to life.

Right about now, the ego is saying, *This gal is delusional. I am being practical, living within my means. I am following the rules and being a good person.* That is what living the illusion is all about. Doing the same thing year after year and expecting a different result, like joy or happiness, is the definition of insanity. Perhaps you have defined yourself into a corner. The corner has no light and no possibilities. The more you do the same things, the more frightened you become of change.

Decide! Decide if this is enough. *If it is, so be it.* If not, do something different. Ask to be shown greater possibilities. Be willing to cross the line to an expanded life. The field of possibilities is vast.

A woman quit her nine-to-five corporate job and became a trapeze artist. Now, she performs in Las Vegas and is having a blast. Dr. Richard Alpert was plagued his whole life with the notion that there had to be more to life than living the East-Coast, higher-education, fancy-dinner-party, be-successful-with-a-sports-car-and-a-Cessna kind-of-life. So, he went to India, met his guru, and became Ram Dass, servant of love. Through his experience, writing and teaching Alpert, or Ram Dass, has affected millions of lives in the best possible way.

What do you think? Are you willing to explore your possibilities? Have you had any whisperings encouraging you to try something new? Are you willing?

Believe You Can and You Can

If you think you can or if you think you can't, you are right.
Henry Ford

"Believe you can and you can," admonished Reverend Norman Vincent Peale. Poet, Henry David Thoreau indicated that *belief* in an enterprise is the one thing fundamental to its success. Hence, the message: If you have a goal or intention, believe that you can attain it. In fact, believe that, even now, you are in the process of attainment and don't change this belief, no matter what.

There is a story of two brothers, Ben and Dan Newmark of Ladue, Missouri, who chose to live by that adage. They worked together to overcome obstacles to create their dream careers in the film industry. Ben wanted to be an actor and he auditioned a lot. One day, Ben decided that, if no one would hire him as an actor in Hollywood, if he couldn't even get a meeting, let alone an audition, he'd write his own TV series, and that is what he did.

Ben started by recruiting his brother Dan. Together, they churned out a script for a comedy-drama about the young inhabitants of a quirky Los Angeles apartment house. They followed this effort by shooting a pilot called "The Wilton Hilton." In nine days, using digital video and casting their friends as characters, they completed their movie.

"Now what?" What came next was rejection. Lots of it. And advice to "get out of the business." Undaunted and determined, they connected with director Lee Krieger and shot a forty-five-minute comedy. Then they hit another pivotal point. "Now what?"

Again, more negative advice. "Dump it in the waste can. Don't screen it. It would be career suicide." So, of course the brothers did the opposite. They rented a theatre, filled the place with friends, and sent postcard invitations to Hollywood insiders, mostly assistants to agents and producers. The result: three trainees from the mailroom at Creative Artists

Agency, one of Hollywood's top talent agencies, took their film back and showed it to the big guys, who loved it.

Voila! They were signed! Ultimately, the brothers pitched their idea to the C.W. Network and a new television series, "The Wilton," was born.

Meeting challenge and adversity proved to be a great motivator to the Newmark brothers. It caused them to be creative, imaginative and determined. It can work the same way for you. Whatever your obstacles and challenges, as you work with them and through them, you make yourself strong. In time, you become undaunted and, soon, you will realize that you can accomplish anything. That is what will assure that your goals will be fulfilled.

Henry David Thoreau often indicated that belief in an enterprise is the one thing fundamental to its success. So, if you have a goal, believe that you can attain it. Believe that you are, even now, in the process of attainment. Then, let your imagination go and follow your dream. Worst case scenario: it leads to something else. Best case scenario: it takes you right where you want to go.

From Poverty to Achievement

Imagination is more important than knowledge.
For knowledge is limited whereas imagination embraces the entire world, stimulating progress, giving birth to evolution.
Albert Einstein

The educator and writer, Jon Karat-Zin, said, "You can't stop the waves, but you can learn to surf." That statement applies to people who take life as it comes and make something amazing out of it. That would also include those who rise from poverty to achieve great success.

One individual that fits the bill is a woman whose family was so poor that people often brought them food baskets. As a little girl, she was humiliated that her father couldn't support the family. When people showed up with food, she would hide and cry bitterly. It was in her misery that she created the goal that helped her to become successful. Poverty can be a great motivator. It has probably helped more people become successful than any other one factor.

James Cash Penney, the great merchant who created the vast network of J.C. Penney stores, was the seventh of twelve children. He was only eight years old when he started raising pigs to earn money for his clothes. He said that one of his great motivators was adversity. He went on to explain that adversity taught him to never give up, always start over, keep his faith strong, and realize that adversity makes a person strong.

Another fellow, named Al Haake, struggled to achieve his goals and did it in a spectacular way. Haake suffered from acute stuttering. When he was young, other children laughed at him in school. They would call him "Out" at baseball games, just to hear him stutter. It was embarrassing and demoralizing.

Then one afternoon, Haake heard a U.S. senator speak. He said, "Look, you can do anything you want to do, if you believe in yourself." Al Haake wanted to believe he could speak clearly. So, he began putting pebbles in his mouth because he had read that a man named Demosthenes did that and overcame his stuttering problem.

Al Haake *believed.* He worked at it and, ultimately, became a great speaker. He was employed by General Motors Corporation to lecture throughout the country. It was said that he held people spellbound by his clarity, articulation, message and beauty of speech.

Lou Holtz, the famous football coach, offers another interesting story. In 1966, when he was twenty-eight years old, he wrote out 107 "impossible" goals. The goals seemed impossible because Holtz had just lost his job, had no money. His wife, Beth, was expecting their third child. In an attempt to lift her husband's spirits, Beth encouraged him to read *The Magic of Thinking Big* by David J. Schwarz.

The book stated that there are many people who don't do anything special with their lives. Holtz related to that statement, as he felt depleted and totally lacking in motivation. So, he decided to write out 107 goals that he wanted to achieve before he died. Holtz's list included having dinner at the White House, appearing on the Tonight Show, meeting the pope, becoming head coach at Notre Dame, winning a national championship, being coach of the year, landing on an aircraft carrier, making a hole-in-one, and jumping out of an airplane.

Writing the goals was the beginning for Holtz as he got busy working. As of a few years ago, Holtz has achieved eighty-one of those goals, including all the ones listed above. He dined with President Ronald Reagan at the White House, appeared with Johnny Carson on the Tonight show, met the pope, jumped from an airplane, and got two (not one) holes-in-one.

Perhaps you can follow Coach Holtz's example and give yourself permission to dream and start a list. You might even try being unrealistic for a change. The secret to this quest is not what you write down, but that you allow yourself to admit that you would like to climb Mt. Kilimanjaro, endow a university, play the flute in Carnegie Hall, or be a better friend. Acknowledging your dream begins the process of creating it.

There is a principle in quantum physics that states a possibility becomes a reality when it is registered. Registering a possibility is simply acknowledging it. Everyone has the potential to do amazing things. So, register your dream; then let go of it. Put your written goals away. As time moves on, accept every opportunity to proceed in the direction of your goal. As you maneuver forward, so does your goal.

Another principle in quantum physics: once you register your desire, the object and the subject change at the same time. In other words, once you claim your goal, you will change along with the goal. You will find yourself putting forth the activity that ultimately creates your desired reality.

It worked for Lou Holtz, who turned out to be the award-winning coach of the Notre Dame football team, and it will work for you as well.

Activity: Write out at least fifty goals you want to achieve before you die. Or you can set a time limit of ten years. Read these goals over at least once a month. Start checking off the ones you achieve. That will help you to believe in the rest of them. In the Quantum Field, all goals are possibilities. Don't limit yourself.

Courage to Be Free

The power of the imagination created the illusion that my vision went much farther than I could go.
Nelson Mandela

Many people accept fear as part of life. Their list of worries fills pages. They go through life walking around ladders, over cracks, avoiding bad weather, staying away from strangers, and on and on, until paranoid. Yes, there are folks who don't mind living in fear, and there are others who do. If you want to be free of apprehension, dread and fright, read on.

The key to defusing fears is to reduce them through a logical process of confrontation: Label the fear. For example, you have the fear of going broke or running out of money. Decide the logical consequences if this fear were to actually come to fruition. For example, you can't pay the bills: *I would have to downsize house and expenses, get food at the food bank, cut out the cable television, look for other kinds of work, etc.*

Now, follow the line of consequences further. What happens when you can't pay the bills? What is the worst possibility? Example: *The electric and phone services are disconnected. I lose my good credit rating.*

Next, ask yourself, *How would I handle this outcome? What would I do?* Example: *I would light candles, cook on the barbecue grill, eat cold foods. I would make calls from work, pay for purchases with cash, and rebuild my credit rating.*

The point is, you have options. By looking straight at your situation, you discover that you have the capacity to handle the worst-case scenario. By facing it, you not only free yourself of fear, but also realize that it isn't as bad as you thought. In fact, the worst-case scenario is doable. Your freedom to make choices is important. People fight wars over that right. People die for that freedom. You are not going to die because you have options.

The final step is a question: Can you handle the worst possibility? There is little in life that cannot be dealt with when you are resolute and possess fortitude. You find your strength and put it to the test. By answering the questions and tracing the likely results, you will know how to stop worrying.

Once you've reasoned through this process, you have put your fears in proper perspective. It is 99% certain that you will likely never face the worst-case scenario. Nevertheless, it loses its sting when viewed objectively. Once you have accepted your strength to deal with it, get busy doing what has to be done to avoid it.

Activity: Name a fear you have allowed to roam around in your mind. Now start the process. What if you were actually facing that fear? Worse-case proposition? Can you handle it? Keep going. Face the next fear and the next one. On the other side of this exercise is the realization that you are brave, you are imaginative, and you are unstoppable!

Adversity to Triumph

To bring anything into your life, imagine that it's already there.
Richard Bach

In his book, *Illusions*, author Richard Bach says, *Argue for your limitations and they belong to you.* Every day, people not only argue for their limitations, but kick, scream and fight to hold on to them. This is what they sound like: "You have to know the right people to get ahead. Everyone is out to get you. Good jobs are hard to come by. Evil is stronger than good." You get the idea. For those that don't want limitation and negativity, there is another way.

In life, we all make choices. Every day, we see the results of our choices. Those who revel in the vice of negativity find their choices uninviting, restrictive and gray in comparison to those that choose to look on the bright side.

Byron Janis is one of the latter. Considered a child prodigy, he was devoted to his music. He practiced endless hours and played for fifty years. At age 57, after playing a guest appearance at the White House, Janis revealed that he had suffered from arthritis for twelve years. He described his condition as follows: "I cannot make a fist. The right wrist's motion is limited to forty percent. The little finger of the left hand is numb, partially paralyzed and scarred from a childhood accident. The joints of the other nine fingers are fused. There is mobility in only one distal joint, that of the middle finger, left hand."

Despite his problems, Janis endured in his art. He looked for different ways to finger the keys, but he never gave up. By looking for solutions and strategies, he found them. It is a matter of where you put your mind. Janis is yet another example of what can be done when one focuses on a goal and refuses to yield to obstacles.

There are heroes of this sort everywhere. People who don't relate to limitation. They're too busy moving ahead, exploring possibilities. We can do the same. There is opportunity waiting for those brave enough to grasp it. You can argue for your limitations or get busy pushing ahead.

Activity: What crazy idea has been circulating in your head of late? Whether you win or you lose, what step can you take now to move toward your crazy idea? In fact, map out three or four steps and, just for the fun of it, take a step in the direction of your crazy idea. What have you got to lose?

Your Unique Design

This place where you are right now, God circles on a map for you.

Hafiz

Assumption: The reasoning mind is limited because it only draws from your past experiences and what you are aware of intellectually. To live a bigger life, you must move beyond the constraints of the reasoning mind and experience the expansive field of pure potentiality or limitless possibilities.

It is a choice. If you say, *I don't see how that can happen,* you are operating from the reasoning (analytical) mind. In other words, how did Jesus walk on water and Sai Baba manifest jewels from thin air? They operated from a higher reality, a higher vibratory field. They did not limit themselves to what everyone else thought was possible.

The truth is that, what seemed impossible even ten years ago, is available and doable now. That is why considering what seems impossible is rational. Each day, open to the field of pure potentiality and ask: What is possible today? Ask that your next step in achieving your intention be revealed.

Listen! Listen to the signs, symbols, and soul urgings.

Move! Take action as directed. Do not get in your own way. Develop tunnel vision to proceed toward your objective. The pauper can become the prince. The homeless person can graduate college. The secretary can eventually own the company. Everything is possible, in Spirit.

When others say *No*, you say *Yes* and keep going. If necessary, block out the world so you can live solely in Spirit and Knowing. *I decree that this (objective) is done!*

Here are some steps to take when you are seeking your next work adventure. You can use this process for any other intention, as well.

Steps to move forward:

Make a list of all your talents and abilities. Everything you've ever been good at: nurturing, organizing, connecting with people, baking a cake, selling an idea, climbing trees, giving orders, cleaning houses, technology, giving orders, etc.

Set the list aside. That was for your reasoning mind to recognize that you are capable of many things. Now, let go of analysis and figuring things out yourself. In other words, get out of the way.

Sit quietly and open your mind to Spirit and everything that goes with it: the field of pure potentiality and possibilities. Just be in space. Be there until you feel stabilized. By creating space for new possibilities to enter, you are allowing Spirit to provide insight and inspiration. Be still and spacious. Do this over and over and your next step will be revealed.

Visualize the kind of activity that would be fun to call *work*. Recognize that this activity is your true expression and it will generate wages/income. Do *not* concern yourself with *how* it will manifest or when, or who, or any other details. Just enter this picture and *feel* the excitement and fun. Give this exercise five minutes. You can do this twice a day.

Give thanks and let go. Get on with the day and do what is in front of you to do.

Do this again tomorrow and the next day.

Change Paves the Way for Growth

You are never given a wish
without also being given the power to make it true.
However, you may have to work for it.

Many people are afraid of change. Usually this means they are afraid of the unknown. It is generally a matter of not trusting themselves. We may as well make peace with change because it is the one constant in life.

Change means to alter, convert or transform the form or content of something. Change can be as simple as ten dimes for a dollar or as complex as birth, death, marriage, divorce or building, using, and finally decaying and releasing. Since change is the only constant in life, we can count on it. Day moves to night and back again. Spring flows to summer and fall to winter. Every molecule of your body is constantly changing. Blood flows. Your breath rotates in and out. Food is digested, assimilated and eliminated. You sleep and wake in a cycle.

Basically, you have two choices where change is concerned. You can adapt to the process or resist it. In other words, you joyfully greet change or are dragged, kicking and screaming, to new phases of life. Since change is inevitable, it is wise to embrace it with enthusiasm.

For instance, you can choose to grow in health or you can physically deteriorate. You can profit from the opportunities change presents and choose progress over stagnation and decline. Even though many find change difficult, it does make life exciting and provokes evolution.

Entertainer and sausage maker, Jimmy Dean, notes, "I can't change the direction of the wind, but I can adjust my sails to always reach my destination."

President John F. Kennedy confirmed that, "Change is the law of life and those who look only to the past or the present are certain to miss the future."

You can prepare yourself for change by regularly stepping out of your routine. Take physical, mental, and spiritual breaks. This will help you see a broader picture and develop adaptability. Charles Darwin acknowledged that, "It is not the strongest of the species that survive, nor the most intelligent, but the one most responsive to change."

Stay open to the possibilities by avoiding judgment, assumptions, and other ego traps. The ego wants to decry expansion. It does that by trying to control everything, insuring the maintenance of status quo and smallness. When you think such things as, *My way is the only way; This is the way I have always done it; It is the right way,* it is time to set your ego aside so you can grow.

Lastly, commit to learning from everyone and everything. Read, ask questions and explore new experiences, places and people. Take classes, attempt new projects. Life is filled with endless possibilities. Investigate as many as possible. The more information you acquire, the larger your range of choices, the more exciting your life, and the greater your growth. What opportunities for expansion are present in your life right now? Set your fear aside and begin investigating one of them.

Activity: Choose a new activity to try out: a local adventure, new place to eat lunch, join a pickle-ball team, take up a new hobby like surf-boarding, chess, a book club. Start something new. Every day, something new. A new route to work. A new way to be of service. Each small thing moves you to a greater reality.

Change Happens from the Inside Out

All meaningful and lasting change starts first in your imagination, then works its way out.
Albert Einstein

Occasionally, we hear about a rock star or a movie that made it to the top and, just as rapidly, crashed and burned. They *arrived* so quickly that they had not learned to handle the pressure of bright lights. The same thing happens to ordinary folks who transform quickly or climb too fast. Couples who marry or bear children before they are ready, haven't laid the foundation for either and may succumb to failure on both counts. Or businesspeople who overwhelm themselves by stretching too far too fast, often break down under stress.

Change happens from the inside out. We must prepare ourselves psychologically and emotionally for each progressive stage. Skipping steps can be detrimental as each step prepares us for the next one.

Consider the analogy of the baby chick, chipping away at the eggshell to gain freedom. Piece by piece, the shell crumbles. The process, requiring time and effort, affords the chick the opportunity to gain strength and stamina, both necessary to survive in the outside world, its next level of expression. If someone were to help in breaking the shell, it would deny the chick this valuable exercise, undermining the chick's survival. Breaking through the shell is an important element in the process of survival, and success.

You are like the chick, in that each step along your path prepares and strengthens you with experience, skill, tenacity, vision and wisdom. By the time you reach your goal, you are ready for it. Where are you in your process? What shell are you currently breaking through? Are you prepared for the next level of expression? Have you gained sufficient strength, experience, stamina, vision to survive? To succeed?

Activity: Consider your present stage of growth. Can you feel an urge to move forward? If so, what does the next phase look like, feel like? Be still and allow these answers to come to you. When they come, you will know what to do.

Letting Go Is Freedom

I am realistic – I expect miracles.
Wayne Dyer

We've all heard of Kentucky Fried Chicken but many may not know the story behind it. Colonel Harlan Sanders was an Asheville, North Carolina, businessman who owned a restaurant and motel that was destroyed in a fire. He rebuilt his business to house a larger restaurant in which he served his special pressure-fried chicken. As the U.S. entered World War II in 1941, gas was rationed and the tourist trade dried up. Sanders was forced to close his motel and restaurant. From there, he moved about the country, working various jobs, but he never forgot his dream of selling his special fried chicken.

Finally, in 1952, Sanders sold his first franchise of "Kentucky Fried Chicken" to Pete Harman of South Salt Lake, Utah. Harman ran the city's largest restaurants, and when Sanders' fried chicken was added to his menu, sales tripled. That is when it was officially crowned *Kentucky Fried Chicken*, evoking imagery of Southern hospitality.

When new Interstate 75 was built, traffic was diverted from the restaurant. It closed, leaving Sanders with his savings and $105 a month from Social Security. Never to be without an idea, at age 65, Sanders decided to hit the road and visit potential franchisees to sell his special fried-chicken recipe.

His franchise approach was highly successful and, ultimately, KFC became one of the first fast-food chains to expand internationally, opening outlets in Canada and later in England, Mexico and Jamaica. Eventually, it expanded to 600 locations.

Sanders' story is filled with beginnings, endings, detours, and curves in the road. In each instance, he let go of his plan and devised a new one. With each change, he learned new strategies, met influential people, and adjusted strategies to fit his dream. With each event, he grew his skill and confidence as a businessman. That is what letting go is all about. By trusting his gut, Sanders became a wealthy man and put KFC on the international map. Each time he let go and started over, he re-invented himself and, ultimately, became a legend in his time.

There is an art to letting go. From stories such as Colonel Harlan Sanders', we learn this art: knowing what to let go of and when to do it. Some believe that when you have battled a situation long enough and do not feel you are winning over it, it is time to let go. There is merit to that argument. Others say that letting go is a daily activity. That's when you are truly desirous of spiritual partnership. You let go continuously to let Spirit lead the way. There is value in that point of view.

What we deal with in the art of letting go is releasing archaic ways, useless beliefs and habits, and completed relationships. Things that have served their purpose. By continuing to hold onto them, they waste energy. It is about letting go in order to move to the next opportunity and freedom. When a situation, activity, or relationship has completed its tenure and no longer serves a purpose or further involvement restricts movement, it is time to let go and make space for the next idea to take hold.

There are those who remain in situations out of habit. In a sense, they are trapped. The reason they stay is that the ego finds comfort in remaining in the known, even though it is stale and restrictive. As the saying goes, comfort is your enemy. Why? Because it shrinks you.

Because you are familiar with it.

The question is. Do you grow or stay stuck, believing it is comfortable? The next question: What am I keeping myself from by staying in a stale, out-grown situation? What is the opportunity for expansion that awaits my release? What doorway can I walk through by allowing this to end?

Infancy must end so that childhood can begin; childhood must end so you can become an adult. When you have worked at the beginner's level, you must let go to advance to the expert's level. Winter has to end for spring to arrive. Life is progressive and change is constant. The proposition is to see change as advancement, growth, and positive for all concerned.

In our intellectual, rational mindset, change is not viewed as positive. The ego fears change, expansion and beginnings. It also fears freedom. Hence, it is a good idea to consider your predicament. Are you still making buggy whips in a mechanized world? Are you still sending telegrams when you can easily zip off a text message? Are you waiting, snow shovel in hand, while spring flowers are budding?

Letting go of that which is complete is freedom. What is your next step, phase, or bigger picture?

Responsibility Leads to Freedom

> *Remember to look up at the stars and not down at your feet. Try to make sense of what you see and wonder about what makes the Universe exist. Be curious. And however difficult life may seem, there is always something you can do and succeed at. It matters that you don't just give up.*

Many people run and hide when the word *responsibility* is mentioned. Yet, these same folks proclaim unrelenting desire for personal freedom. The notion that responsibility denotes burden, heaviness, and no fun is a falsehood. Responsibility is the medium through which you create personal freedom.

We've all heard the edict: *The truth will set you free.* It could be clarified further by adding: *Applying the truth of responsibility will set you free.* In our society, we've been raised to think that it is our job to make our parents proud, our boss rich, our children smart, and get everyone to like us. To that end, we merrily walk along life's path only to discover tremendous struggle. It's not easy getting people to be what you want them to be: rich, smart, proud, etc. So, when we venture upon an uncooperative soul, it becomes our *job* to *fix* that person. Repairing someone else is a lot harder than it might initially appear, because you have no power or control in changing another person. If they choose to remain damaged, wounded or unchanged, you are doomed to failure.

Concentrating on others' problems is a direct path to victimhood. For if you feel responsible for others' conditions, it follows that you feel someone else is responsible for yours. There you are, stuck waiting for someone to arrive to fix your life. The idea that completeness (wholeness/perfection) can be wantonly thrust upon a person, implies life is a dice game, a chance draw of the cards, a bet at the races, and leaves little hope in achieving through one's own efforts.

Victims are so busy bemoaning life's unfairness that they don't have time to look at themselves. (This is a calculated and convenient preoccupation.) They seek magic, like meeting the right people, being in the right place to receive their goodies from others. *How come some lady was sitting on that bar stool in that drug store being discovered as a movie star and not me?* Interpretation? *Life is unfair. I'm more deserving than her.*

Victims are so busy commiserating, they can't see that the world is teeming with opportunity. There are unlimited opportunities to meet people, train and educate yourself, move up on the professional ladder, learn interpersonal, entrepreneurial or creative skills, try new foods, have inspiring experiences, go new places, stretch yourself through growth-oriented risks.

The core of the issue is this: What is your real responsibility? The answer is simple. You are responsible to and for yourself. To be the kind of person you want to be. To go for the life experience you desire. To express and share the love you have. That's it!

When we spend our time burdening ourselves by fixing other's mistakes rather than learning from our own, we are giving someone a fish, rather than teaching them how to fish. Soon, we are running in sixteen directions, trying to supply nourishment to all the people with sad looks on their faces. You are free when you can say, *There's the bait bucket. Take what you want and go for it. I have trust that you can pull in fish (jobs, friends, money, health, joy).*

If you do for someone something they can do for themselves, you become part of the problem. The solution: *Let Go*!

Your responsibility is to yourself. *Ah,* you say, *that is selfish.* Indeed, you are right. It is selfish to put your attention on yourself. Yet, you are the only person you can do anything about. And the world probably won't honor you for that. So, you better do the applauding. Hold your head high and be proud of your sacred selfish, practical, realistic approach to life. As you assume responsibility for your life, you enrich and inspire everyone around you.

By addressing yourself as your primary assignment (responsibility, not burden), you are providing an unselfish service. You offer a model, example, teacher, inspiration and encouragement to everyone and freedom to yourself.

Activity: How are you nurturing yourself now? How are you providing yourself inspiration? How are you taking care of your body-vehicle? In what way are you addressing your emotional needs? Spiritual needs?

Sounds like a lot of work, right? Yes, it is, and you have signed up for it by showing up in the world. Get ready! Make a plan. Once you remove everyone else from your worry list and get started with your own life, the plan will fall into place.

Truth Power

Life shrinks or expands in proportion to one's courage.
Anais Nin

If you have ever fallen flat on your face or felt like a failure, you might want to remember this story because it involves a fellow who had the same experience. He was the pride of his wealthy parents who provided every advantage, including the best schools, a law degree and even introductions to prominent people. Yet, beyond that, it was up to him to prove his mettle by becoming a capable lawyer, and this guy had a terrible time in the courtroom. Easily overwhelmed, he was unable to stand up to opposition. His shyness and fear brought him to a wretched state of suffering. Finally, he realized that there were people far worse off than he. That is when he began to turn himself around, for it was then that he realized he could help alleviate the distress of others.

It was at this point, when he took his focus off his own miseries that he began developing a new philosophy called *Truth Power*. Through this philosophy, he was able to lead his native India to independence from the unfair treatments practiced under British law. His name was Mohandas Gandhi, later to be known as Mahatma Gandhi (great man).

In developing the philosophy of Truth Power, Gandhi incorporated the concepts he had learned as a child when his father had educated him in the importance of courage, generosity and unwavering adherence to the principles of morality and truth. At the same time, his mother demonstrated gentleness, modesty, consideration, and the flexible strength that enables one to overcome through yielding. Both parents taught that if he wanted positive results, he must be positive, and that goodness, demonstrated persistently, triumphs over evil, even though it may seem to take time.

Gandhi claimed that Truth Power would overcome opponents by

changing them with respectful patient persistence, transforming them, not annihilating them. Repeatedly, he was told it would not work. Again and again, despite overwhelming odds, it did. In India, it led to democratic reforms: unification of political territories, the end of civil war, revival of home industries, emancipation of the *untouchables* from an unjust caste system, and freedom for the nation from British rule.

What do you think could happen if everyone decided to incorporate the principles of Truth Power in their world?

Vertical or Horizontal Growth - Your Choice!

Don't limit yourself.
Many people limit themselves to what they think they can do.
You can go as far as your mind lets you.
What you believe, remember, you can achieve.
Mary Kay Ash

Hopefully, everyone is growing in some way or other. Some jump into life with great enthusiasm because they have abundant curiosity and want to know things. Others do not consider life as a growth process but something to get through, something to survive. In that case, no particular insight is achieved. Not even survival. Life is just a series of experiences. Growth occurs in the unaware mind with no particular insight achieved. Yet, there is always potential for growth.

There are indeed two types of growth. The first one is horizontal or linear growth. This means you develop mentally, emotionally, and spiritually unconsciously. You are on a horizontal trajectory, going from birth to death, developing characteristics and managing responsibility as you try to feel secure. Of course, security is fleeting because nothing remains the same in the material world.

The second growth path is vertical, which means you address life as an opportunity to develop deep understanding and awareness. You look beyond experiences to find their meaning. You consciously direct your mind toward spiritual connection. With sincerity and openness, you ask the question: *Why?* You listen and watch for your answer. Your life is about what is behind the surface, and you look for the Light in every person and situation.

Generally, vertical growth is hard earned because you are not walking a traditional path, like the great masters Jesus, Buddha, Mahatma Gandhi, Martin Luther King, Jr. Vertical growth involves taking full responsibility for everything that happens in your life. In effect, you grab the reins and live life purposely with the goal of enlightenment. Life is an opportunity to fully express as a spiritual being with vision and insight.

To understand the difference between these two choices, draw a horizontal line on a piece of paper. This line represents horizontal or linear growth. It is a timeline: birth, growing up with friends and family, school, relationships, job/career, learning through responsibility and death.

Next, cross this line with a vertical line, so that the two lines look like a cross. This line represents vertical growth. That is to say, it represents spiritual growth.

It is true we may live many similar lives in a particular habit pattern and, sometimes, we grow in kindness and wisdom through horizontal growth. We add skills and understanding and become more aware and expressive. This illustrates linear progression. It is experiential from a 3-D five-sensory journey.

Vertical growth is the soul seeking itself. It is a path set on enlightenment, on finding your spiritual home. Therefore, to grow vertically is a choice and it is done with conscious intent.

Chapter 9: Inspiration and Conclusion

Loving-Kindness

Not how long, but how well you have lived is the main thing.
Seneca

Buddhists have a term for the quality of boundless friendship toward oneself or others. It is *metta.* It refers to being loving and kind. Practicing this principle of loving-kindness, particularly toward people we don't know, expands our innate capacity for connecting. Through the quality of loving-kindness, we are able to break the habit of apathy or judgment that generates a feeling of separation from others. Separation fosters fear and prejudice.

Every person has the potential for friendship and kindness. It exists within everyone, no matter what dire experiences one has had. This capacity cannot be destroyed, although it can be ignored or neglected.

The way you re-discover your capability is to take a positive interest in people. We're often running through life so fast that we overlook or discount the people we see in everyday circumstances. They don't even register. Yet relationships make up the fiber of our lives and constitute our greatest challenge and opportunity for growth.

Practice being attentive. Start with someone you don't really know. As you pay attention, you will learn things about the person (and yourself). Next hold that person in your heart and feel genuine warmth for him or her. At the same time, mentally wish that person well. In short notice, you will no longer feel like a stranger. Your world will begin to change. You no longer feel alone. Your life feels suddenly freer.

The next step is to practice with someone you feel ambivalent toward. Aha! It gets easier! With success, you get bolder, which ultimately leads you to people with whom you're in conflict. Choose someone you have injured or who has hurt you. With tenacity, you will get past the lightning bolts of anger. In time, your rage dissipates and you discover increased energy and deeper love than you had ever imagined. As your attention opens to the people you formerly dismissed, your world expands along with your connection to yourself. Work on your ability to be kind and loving. You will discover how truly unlimited and safe you are.

Ask for Help!

The purpose of our lives is to be happy.
Dalai Lama

If you put a buzzard in a pen six or eight feet square, and leave it entirely open at the top, the bird, in spite of its ability to fly, will be an absolute prisoner. The reason is that a buzzard always begins flight from the ground with a run of ten or twelve feet. Without its predetermined space to run it will not even attempt to fly, but will remain a prisoner for life in a small jail with no top.

We humans are the same. Often, we insist that, unless success comes to us in an exact way, based on a preconceived idea held in the mind, we become a prisoner of our present environment and past mistakes. There could be a dozen open doors while we stand at the closed, locked one, waiting an entire lifetime for it to open.

The ordinary bat that flies around at night is a remarkable lithe creature in the air, but it cannot take off from a level place. If it is placed on flat ground, all it can do is shuffle about helplessly and, no doubt, painfully. Until it can reach a slight elevation from which to toss itself into the air, it is grounded. Then, at once, it takes off like a flash.

Often in life, we must reinvent ourselves so that we can take off from any
angle or position. To the individual who does not know how to rise up again, God is a great resource. God will show you how to fly above adversity that has held you down for too long.

A bumblebee, if dropped into an open tumbler, will stay there, helpless and disheartened, until someone takes it out. It never sees the means of escape at the top, but persists in trying to find a way out through the sides of the tumbler. It will seek a way where none exists until it is exhausted and destroyed.

People exhibit the same phenomena. They will argue for their limitations and beat their head against a wall of continued ineffective activity or habit, not going anywhere because they have decided it is the right way. They will choose to stay stuck in an approach that doesn't work, rather than admit that what they are doing isn't working. They will avoid lifting their vision to try a new way, stepping out of their comfort zone or taking a leap of faith.

This is why I encourage a spiritual approach to problem-solving. Spirit knows no limitation but does require you to look with different eyes, try something new, approach from another angle. Spiritual study and meditation change you. You become lighter, more observant, calmer and more courageous. God does not change as God is changeless, always loving and willing to assist. But you must *ask.* Ask and the door will be opened. Seek and you will find.

Instead of beating your head against the glass jar when the top is wide open, ask for help and be willing to accept the assistance that shows up. *I am up against the wall and what I am doing is not working. I move my own self out of the way and open to You, God!* Then, wait and listen. Watch for signs, for the right people to show up, for an opportunity to present itself. Be open and humble. Take the next step as it appears.

There are lots of people like the buzzard, the bat, and the bee. They struggle with their problems and frustrations, not realizing that the answer is right there *above* their small, closely-held concepts, their it-is-supposed-to-happen-this-way mindset. If you find yourself in a similar position, turn your attention inward to your heart and speak sincerely. Ask for the help you have been promised and allow yourself to raise your wings to the ethers of divine inspiration. Your answer will come in ways you may not expect, but it will come. Do what the bee, the buzzard and the bat did not consider and open to a new possibility. Look beyond your fixed mindset and leap into the unknown, knowing that you are never alone. By being receptive, your way will be shown.

No Time

Being limited in time can be kryptonite for creativity.

Geniuses Steve Jobs and Albert Einstein, as creative beings, agreed on the notion of taking time to do nothing. They both spent regular periods of time pondering possibilities and poking around with divergent ideas, allowing the neuroscience of creativity to occur while doing nothing in particular. They were also quite expert in putting their ideas into practice. Their "no time" was defined as a vast stretch of emptiness whereby they could relax and let the big picture or innovative ideas come to light. It required removing themselves from the hustle and bustle of everyday life. By indulging in "no time," they were able to change the world.

In the same way, giving yourself time to patiently do nothing can be a powerful ingredient in allowing creative juices to flow. Many successful people find hanging out on the golf course or taking a drive into the country a way to release pressure and plumb their minds for their next creative impulse or step.

Activity: Map out a two-hour period every morning for time to be, ponder, contemplate and meditate. Note the changes that occur in your creative expression.

Conclusion - Connecting with the Divine

I am ending this book the way I started it with a quote from the Bible:

You are Gods.

Mark 4:4

Throughout this manuscript, I have sought to inspire change in the reader. Change opens a threshold to transformation, and transformation leads to expansion and Highest Intelligence. Ultimately, the connection we seek is with the divine. Making a connection of that sort is profound and requires a vast adjustment in letting go of negatives, like fear, anger, resentment, shame and guilt. Basically, all unconstructive attitudes. Why? Because to experience the grace of God, we must lift our energy and vision to meet God. We must become love.

In the chapter on wisdom, you have found many hints on how to do that. In the chapter on intuition, you will discover ways to connect with the Presence of God and hear the guiding messages that come through daily. But there is a price to pay to achieve that treasured gift. The payment is discipline, which includes letting go of small-mindedness and judgment. Small-mindedness and judgment do not enrich you, yet they are cultural habits and, until the ego is dissolved to where there is no longer ego competition for who is right and who is best, we will be tempted to hold on to societal habits that limit and suppress our dynamic potential for growth.

My desire for you is that you explore the practices outlined in this book and develop mental discipline and strength, along with the ability to fix on your objective until it is manifest. I also wish for you the peace that goes beyond understanding.

I offer my great appreciation to all who choose to travel this path of self-mastery. This is how we will change the world. We are designed to be the masters of our fate. Now is the time!

Last Words...

For eons, people have sought truth, a deeper meaning to life, what it is really all about? Going through the experience in a robotic trance, moving from one experience to the next without definition or purpose, feels empty, meaningless. What's the point?

This is the quandary in which we find ourselves. We want higher purpose, deeper meaning, and transcendence. It is a drive and a purpose. It has been my quest for meaning. The intellect (head) can only take us a little way and then we must go to the heart. The heart takes us deeper, to the soul.

Opening your heart requires dedication and love. You must give up (surrender) old patterns of anger, self-centeredness, judgment and criticism to see the beauty in all that is. Beauty in soul, in life, and in each person, including yourself.

In truth, all is perfect right now because you are supplied with the tools you need on this journey of self-discovery. Whatever it takes to get you there will be provided. Resist and it is harder. Accept and you find comfort in this knowing.

If you must journey to the depths of despair, there is beauty there. It may be the way to burn off old ways and useless beliefs. Are you willing to experience it? In fact, to plumb the depths of your being is to break through layers of egoic illusion to ultimately surrender to something greater. In the process, you come to recognize that the small individual self is nothing and is only of use when surrendered to the guidance of a greater force: the Source.

That is the journey. It is not for the faint of heart, for you will be tested. How committed are you in your quest? From a rough stone you will be polished into a magnificent diamond of beauty and possibility. The process involves pressure. Nothing you can't handle.

The messages in this book are to provide insight and encouragement. If you can, read this book with your heart instead of your intellect. Feel it and you will understand.

The bottom line…authenticity means being who you really are and what is that? You are the energy of the Universe and the truth of your being is in your heart. The mind wants to tell you otherwise, but the mind is only a vehicle that the consciousness of who you are is using to experience in the outer world.

The material world is also a vehicle filled with symbols and nothing more. It is a schoolroom where you can act out your karmic awareness until to exhaust the ego, personality, and your concocted needs and wants. It is then that resistance dissolves and you can sink gratefully into the love that you are.

The external world is just a mirror. It reflects to you through your friends, colleagues, family and circumstances. Your level of willingness and resistance is the indicator and determiner of what must be, because the entire earth journey is about waking up. Just as Buddha said, *I am awake.* We, too, are on a journey to awake. We have been asleep and mesmerized by the drama and adventure of earth life. When we find it taxing enough, we turn within and it is there that we discover the love we seek. Will we miss the drama? No, because by the time we turn to face the reality of love, we will be ready.

There is no rush. You will arrive at the right moment for you, and the suffering you endure as you travel the road to enlightenment (awakening) is to prepare you, to wear you out with all the nonsense of the fear-based ego mind. No matter what, you are never abandoned. You are always loved. Can you see with new eyes that everything has been stacked in your favor? Every event, every person has been a guide. All have been guiding you home.

Bless you on your journey. May this book provide nourishment, inspiration and assistance as you travel your path.

Meditation Practice - Getting Started

Albert Einstein, Mahatma Gandhi, the Dalai Lama, Deepak Chopra, Steve Jobs, and Thomas Edison, among many others, all supported the practice of meditation as a way to still the mind and reach higher realms of inspiration and consciousness. That is the message I close with in this book. The mind is your property. What you do with it is your salvation or detriment. Use it well. In other words, you control it. Don't let it control you. It is yours to use as a tool for greater awareness and peace.

To bring forth the greatest inspiration and expansion, I close with a meditation practice that you can use to absorb the messages in this book and merge with them.

Meditation Technique

I suggest you take one of the articles from this book, or you can even open the book to something and consider that Spirit picked it for you, and use it as the meditation subject. That means, you will concentrate on the subject of the article as you move into meditation. This is a consciousness-building exercise.

With the subject in mind, close your eyes while *seated* in a comfortable position with your back straight and your head up. Best to use a straight-back chair for this practice because you want to stay awake and aware. Begin by taking several slow deep breaths. Consider that when you inhale, you are taking in energy, and when you exhale, you are releasing used energy. With each breathe, relax deeply.

When you have reached a quiet, relaxed state, hold your subject in mind. Peace, Flow, God, Gratitude, Kindness, whatever. Observe the subject. Feel it. Ask Spirit to define it, expand it, enliven it. Stay focused. If you drift away from the subject, just recognize it and refocus.

Stay with this practice for ten minutes. When you are finished, take your notebook and write whatever you felt during this meditation. Write whatever came to your mind.

My suggestion is that you stay with the same subject for a week of daily meditation. If you consider this practice a time of self-service, you will discover it to be refreshing, fulfilling and peaceful. It will expand your Presence!

About Jean Walters

Jean Walters is a St. Louis based teacher of Self-Empowerment principles. She has been in the field of personal growth for forty years, has studied metaphysics extensively, and applies Universal principles to every area of her life.

In her practice, she helps clients sort through relationships, career choices, experiences, decisions, lessons to learn, and a path to follow. Along the way, she has developed classes, books, and videos to educate students and truth seekers in universal law, meditation, dreams and their value, the practicality of personal growth, and various personal-empowerment methods to develop spiritually.

During her career, she has written nine books, published numerous free-lance articles, as well as written weekly and monthly columns in major newspapers and publications. Her syndicated radio show, *Positive Moments*, was broadcast on 110 stations around the nation. She has been a featured guest on radio, television, and podcasts. Additionally, Walters has lectured, designed, and taught classes and workshops for many organizations, colleges, universities and businesses.

Presently, she has a private practice as a Transformational Coach in St. Louis, Missouri. Her personal-growth classes are taught at various locations, including the St. Louis Community College. Also, for over thirty years, she has provided over 35,000 Akashic (psychic) readings to those seeking personal insight concerning life-purpose, relationships, health, career, and various other dynamics of life.

Her Mission Statement: To encourage, assist, and guide individuals to live freely and express from their Highest Selves.

Check Out Jean's Resources

Website:
http://www.spiritualtransformation.com

Blog:
http://www.spiritualtransformation.com/blog

Amazon.com author page:
https://www.amazon.com/Jean-Walters/e/B00MGBVDJS/

Video library:
YouTube: Jean Walters
https://www.youtube.com/channel/UCnVjf1AAnzZxi56reIkif3g
https://www.youtube.com/channel/UCroNsq_NFvpiiG8bja44Kyg

Meditation Class:
https://www.udemy.com/course/the-art-of-meditation-how-and-why

Newsletter: (specials, information on upcoming classes and inspirational pick me-ups. YES YOU CAN articles, and other interesting tidbits):
http://www.spiritualtransformation.com/subscribe.php

Email Address (for questions or more information):
jean@spiritualtransformation.com

Social media:
twitter.com/LightandJoy
facebook.com/SpiritualTransformation-115925819587
linkedin.com/in/jean-walters-58b172

Other Books Written by Jean Walters

Set Yourself Free: *Live the Life YOU Were Meant to Live*

Be Outrageous*: Do the Impossible – Others have and you can too! (Live Your Passion)*

The Power of KNOWING: *8-Step Guide to Open Your Intuitive Channel and Live in Highest Consciousness*

The Journey from Anxiety to Peace: *Practical Steps to Handle Fear, Embrace Struggle and Eliminate Worry to Become Happy and Free*

The Magic and Mystery of Dreams: The Ultimate Handbook for Interpreting Day and Night Drams and the Symbols in Your Life

Look Mom, I'm Flying (For children and the child within you)

Dream Journal

Choosing Health: *You have a right to health; are you willing to claim it!*

Made in the USA
Monee, IL
28 April 2024

57634271R00134